Donald R. Koepke, MDiv, BCC
Editor

Ministering to Older Adults: The Building Blocks

Ministering to Older Adults: The Building Blocks has been co-published simultaneously as *Journal of Religion, Spirituality & Aging,* Volume 17, Numbers 3/4 2005.

Pre-publication
REVIEWS,
COMMENTARIES,
EVALUATIONS . . .

More Pre-publication
REVIEWS, COMMENTARIES, EVALUATIONS . . .

"This book PROVIDES A DEFINITIVE STEP-BY-STEP PROCESS for designing congregational older adult ministries with an emphasis on meeting the spiritual needs of older adults. I would recommend this book to any congregation that is truly committed to older adult ministry."

Greg Cohen, BS
Ordained Elder, Presbyterian Church
Associate, Older Adult Ministries
Mission Program and Funding

"AN EXCELLENT RESOURCE . . . PROVIDES A COMPREHENSIVE, IN-DEPTH UNDERSTANDING of the unique role churches can play in meeting the spiritual needs of older adults. . . . Serves as a touchstone to evaluate what you are doing, and how you can improve your ministry. I am excited and looking forward to putting this well-written volume in the hands of our OWLS (Older Wiser Lutherans) Ministry Team. . . . Presents tools that will be invaluable . . . and a wealth of resources that will make our tasks easier."

Pastor Helen Leisenberg, MDiv
Director of Seniors Ministry
Ascension Lutheran Church
Rancho Palos Verdes, California

"This book is RICH WITH EXAMPLES, SUGGESTIONS, TOOLS, AND COMPELLING QUESTIONS about older adult ministry, and these 'building blocks' are held together by the strong mortar of theory and theology. The authors speak from experience, learning, and their own spiritual framework to provide insight and challenges to the reader. Practical applications, concrete examples, and reproducible tools make this a complete 'how-to' manual. This is a book that will not sit on the shelf, but will be worn and earmarked with frequent use."

Sharon Adkins, RN, MSN
Director, Center for Parish Nursing
and Health Ministries
Vanderbilt University Medical Center

Ministering to Older Adults: The Building Blocks

Ministering to Older Adults: The Building Blocks has been co-published simultaneously as *Journal of Religion, Spirituality & Aging,* Volume 17, Numbers 3/4 2005.

Monographic Separates from the *Journal of Religion, Spirituality & Aging*™

For additional information on these and other Haworth Press titles, including descriptions, tables of contents, reviews, and prices, use the QuickSearch catalog at http://www.HaworthPress.com.

The *Journal of Religion, Spirituality & Aging*™ is the successor title to *Journal of Religious Gerontology** which changed title after Vol. 16, No. 3/4, 2004 and *Journal of Religion & Aging*** which changed title after Vol. 6, No. 3/4, 1989. *Journal of Religion, Spirituality & Aging*™ under its new title, begins with Vol. 17, No. 1/2, 2004.

Ministering to Older Adults: The Building Blocks, edited by Donald R. Koepke, MDiv, BCC (Vol. 17, No. 3/4, 2005). *A step-by-step guide for the development of an older adult ministry that focuses on the unique needs of each congregation and uses the unique resources found within that congregation.*

Spiritual Assessment and Interventions with Older Adults: Current Directions and Applications, edited by Mark Brennan, PhD, and Deborah Heiser, PhD (Vol. 17, No. 1/2, 2004). *An overview of the state of the art and new developments in the development and implementation of spiritual interventions for older adults.*

Spirituality of Later Life: On Humor and Despair, edited by Rev. Elizabeth MacKinlay, PhD, RN* (Vol. 16, No. 3/4, 2004). *"I found the content THOUGHT-PROVOKING AND RICH IN IDEAS. This book is an important and stimulating contribution to the study of spirituality and aging. It deserves careful attention from pastors, chaplains, and religious workers serving older adults." (Richard H. Genzler, Jr., DMin, CSA, Director, Center on Aging & Older Adult Ministries, General Board of Discipleship of The United Methodist Church)*

Faith-Based Initiatives and Aging Services, edited by F. Ellen Netting, PhD, and James W. Ellor, PhD* (Vol. 16, No. 1/2, 2004). *A guide to the key issues in the development and implementation of faith-based programs as defined by both community agencies and the Center for Faith-Based and Community Initiatives.*

Practical Theology for Aging, edited by Rev. Derrel R. Watkins, PhD* (Vol. 15, No. 1/2, 2003). *"THOUGHT-PROVOKING, ENLIGHTENING, INSIGHTFUL, AND PRACTICAL. As I read through the book, I repeatedly found myself thinking, 'what AN EXCELLENT SUPPLEMENTAL TEXT for the Introduction to Gerontology course.' AN EXCELLENT TRAINING RESOURCE for health care providers working with older adults, as well as religious leaders of all denominations as they seek to enhance their pastoral care programs with older adults." (Patricia Gleason-Wynn, PhD, Lecturer, School of Social Work, Baylor University)*

New Directions in the Study of Late Life Religiousness and Spirituality, edited by Susan H. McFadden, PhD, Mark Brennan, PhD, and Julie Hicks Patrick, PhD* (Vol. 14, No. 1, 2/3, 2003). *"Refreshing. . . . encouraging. . . . This book has given us a gift of evolving thoughts and perspectives on religion and spirituality in the later years of life. . . . Of interest not only to university students, researchers, and scholars, but also to those who provide services to the aged." (James Birren, PhD, Associate Director, UCLA Center on Aging)*

Aging Spirituality and Pastoral Care: A Multi-National Perspective, edited by Rev. Elizabeth MacKinlay, RN, PhD, Rev. James W. Ellor, PhD, DMin, DCSW, and Rev. Stephen Pickard, PhD* (Vol. 12, No. 3/4, 2001). *"Comprehensive . . . The authors are not just thinkers and scholars. They speak from decades of practical expertise with the aged, demented, and dying." (Bishop Tom Frame, PhD, Lecturer in Public Theology, St. Mark's National Theological Centre, Canberra, Australia)*

Religion and Aging: An Anthology of the Poppele Papers, edited by Derrel R. Watkins, PhD, MSW, MRE* (Vol. 12, No. 2, 2001). *"Within these pages, the new ministry leader is supplied with the core prerequisites for effective older adult ministry and the more experienced leader is provided with an opportunity to reconnect with timeless foundational principles. Insights into the* *interior of the aging experience, field-tested and proven techniques and ministry principles, theological rationale for adult care giving, Biblical perspectives on aging, and philosophic and spiritual insights into the aging process." (Dennis R. Myers, LMSW-ACP, Director, Baccalaureate Studies in Social Work, Baylor University, Waco, Texas)*

Aging in Chinese Society: A Holistic Approach to the Experience of Aging in Taiwan and Singapore, edited by Homer Jernigan and Margaret Jernigan* (Vol. 8, No. 3, 1992). *"A vivid introduction to aging in these societies. . . . Case studies illustrate the interaction of religion, personality, immigration, modernization, and aging." (Clinical Gerontologist)*

Spiritual Maturity in the Later Years, edited by James J. Seeber* (Vol. 7, No. 1/2, 1991). *"An excellent introduction to the burgeoning field of gerontology and religion." (Southwestern Journal of Theology)*

Gerontology in Theological Education: Local Program Development, edited by Barbara Payne and Earl D. C. Brewer** (Vol. 6, No. 3/4, 1989). *"Directly relevant to gerontological education in other contexts and to applications in the educational programs and other work of church congregations and community agencies for the aging." (The Newsletter of the Christian Sociological Society)*

Gerontology in Theological Education, edited by Barbara Payne and Earl D. C. Brewer** (Vol. 6, No. 1/2, 1989). *"An excellent resource for seminaries and anyone interested in the role of the church in the lives of older persons . . . must for all libraries." (David Maldonado, DSW, Associate Professor of Church & Society, Southern Methodist University, Perkins School of Theology)*

Religion, Aging and Health: A Global Perspective, compiled by the World Health Organization, edited by William M. Clements** (Vol. 4, No. 3/4, 1989). *"Fills a long-standing gap in gerontological literature. This book presents an overview of the interrelationship of religion, aging, and health from the perspective of the world's major faith traditions that is not available elsewhere . . . " (Stephen Sapp, PhD, Associate Professor of Religious Studies, University of Miami, Coral Gables, Florida)*

New Directions in Religion and Aging, edited by David B. Oliver** (Vol. 3, No. 1/2, 1987). *"This book is a telescope enabling us to see the future. The data of the present provides a solid foundation for seeing the future." (Dr. Nathan Kollar, Professor of Religious Studies and Founding Chair, Department of Gerontology, St. John Fisher College; Adjunct Professor of Ministerial Theology, St. Bernard's Institute)*

The Role of the Church in Aging, Volume 3: Programs and Services for Seniors, edited by Michael C. Hendrickson** (Vol. 2, No. 4, 1987). *Experts explore an array of successful programs for the elderly that have been implemented throughout the United States in order to meet the social, emotional, religious, and health needs of the elderly.*

The Role of the Church in Aging, Volume 2: Implications for Practice and Service, edited by Michael C. Hendrickson** (Vol. 2, No. 3, 1986). *"Filled with important insight and state-of-the-art concepts that reflect the cutting edge of thinking among religion and aging professionals." (Rev. James W. Ellor, DMin, AM, CSW, ACSW, Associate Professor, Department Chair, Human Service Department, National College of Education, Lombard, Illinois)*

The Role of the Church in Aging, Volume 1: Implications for Policy and Action, edited by Michael C. Hendrickson** (Vol. 2, No. 1/2, 1986). *Reviews the current status of the religious sector's involvement in the field of aging and identifies a series of strategic responses for future policy and action.*

Published by

The Haworth Pastoral Press, 10 Alice Street, Binghamton, NY 13904-1580 USA

The Haworth Pastoral Press is an imprint of The Haworth Press, Inc., 10 Alice Street, Binghamton, NY 13904-1580 USA.

Ministering to Older Adults: The Building Blocks has been co-published simultaneously as *Journal of Religion, Spirituality & Aging,* Volume 17, Numbers 3/4 2005.

The development, preparation, and publication of this work has been undertaken with great care. However, the publisher, employees, editors, and agents of The Haworth Press and all imprints of The Haworth Press, Inc., including The Haworth Medical Press® and Pharmaceutical Products Press®, are not responsible for any errors contained herein or for consequences that may ensue from use of materials or information contained in this work. Opinions expressed by the author(s) are not necessarily those of The Haworth Press, Inc.

Cover design by Lora Wiggins

Library of Congress Cataloging-in-Publication Data

Ministering to older adults: the building blocks/Donald R. Koepke, editor.
    p. cm.
    " . . . has ben co-published simultaneously as Journal of religion, spirituality & aging, Volume 17, Numbers 3/4 2005."
    Includes bibliographical references and index.
    ISBN-13: 978-0-7890-3048-1 (hardcover: alk. paper)
    ISBN-10: 0-7890-3048-9 (hardcover: alk. paper)
    ISBN-13: 978-0-7890-3049-8 (pbk.: alk. paper)
    ISBN-10: 0-7890-3049-7 (pbk.: alk. paper)
    1. Church work with older people. 2. Aging–Religious aspects–Christianity. I. Koepke, Donald R. II. Journal of religion, spirituality & aging.
    BV4435.M54 2005
    259´.3–dc22
                                                      2005011144

Ministering to Older Adults:
The Building Blocks

Donald R. Koepke, MDiv, BCC
Editor

Ministering to Older Adults: The Building Blocks has been co-published simultaneously as *Journal of Religion, Spirituality & Aging,* Volume 17, Numbers 3/4 2005.

The Haworth Pastoral Press®
An Imprint of The Haworth Press, Inc.

New York • London • Victoria (AU)
www.HaworthPress.com

Indexing, Abstracting & Website/Internet Coverage

This section provides you with a list of major indexing & abstracting services and other tools for bibliographic access. That is to say, each service began covering this periodical during the year noted in the right column. Most Websites which are listed below have indicated that they will either post, disseminate, compile, archive, cite or alert their own Website users with research-based content from this work. (This list is as current as the copyright date of this publication.)

(continued)

- *Family Index Database <http://www.familyscholar.com>* 1995
- *Google <http://www.google.com>* 2004
- *Google Scholar <http://scholar.google.com>* 2004
- *Guide to Social Science & Religion in Periodical Literature* 2000
- *Haworth Document Delivery Center <http://www.HaworthPress.com/journals/dds.asp>* 1991
- *Human Resources Abstracts (HRA)* 1991
- *IBZ International Bibliography of Periodical Literature <http://www.saur.de>* 1994
- *Index Guide to College Journals (core list compiled by integrating 48 indexes frequently used to support undergraduate programs in small to medium sized libraries)* 1999
- *Index to Jewish Periodicals <http://www.jewishperiodicals.com>* 2001
- *Internationale Bibliographie der geistes- und sozialwissenschaftlichen Zeitschriftenliteratur . . . See IBZ <http://www.saur.de>* 1994
- *Links@Ovid (via CrossRef targeted DOI links) <http://www.ovid.com>* 2005
- *Magazines for Libraries (Katz) . . . (see 2003 edition)* 2003
- *New Literature on Old Age <http://www.cpa.org.uk>* 1995
- *Orere Source, The (Pastoral Abstracts)* 1998
- *Ovid Linksolver (open URL link resolver via CrossRef targeted DOI links <http://www.linksolver.com>* 2005
- *Pastoral Abstracts (The Journal of Pastoral Care & Counseling) <http://www.jpcp.org>* 1998
- *Psychological Abstracts (PsycINFO) <http://www.apa.org>* 2000
- *Religious & Theological Abstracts <http://www.rtabst.org>* 1991
- *Sage Family Studies Abstracts (SFSA)* 1995
- *Sage Urban Studies Abstracts (SUSA)* 1995
- *Social Services Abstracts <http://www.csa.com>* 1991
- *Social Work Abstracts <http://www.silverplatter.com/catalog/swab.htm>* 1991
- *Sociological Abstracts (SA) <http://www.csa.com>* 1991
- *Theology Digest (also made available on CD-ROM)* 1992
- *Violence and Abuse Abstracts: A Review of Current Literature on Interpersonal Violence (VAA)* 1995
- *zetoc <http://zetoc.mimas.ac.uk>* 2004

* **Exact start date to come.**

Special Bibliographic Notes related to special journal issues
(separates) and indexing/abstracting:

- indexing/abstracting services in this list will also cover material in any "separate" that is co-published simultaneously with Haworth's special thematic journal issue or DocuSerial. Indexing/abstracting usually covers material at the article/chapter level.
- monographic co-editions are intended for either non-subscribers or libraries which intend to purchase a second copy for their circulating collections.
- monographic co-editions are reported to all jobbers/wholesalers/approval plans. The source journal is listed as the "series" to assist the prevention of duplicate purchasing in the same manner utilized for books-in-series.
- to facilitate user/access services all indexing/abstracting services are encouraged to utilize the co-indexing entry note indicated at the bottom of the first page of each article/chapter/contribution.
- this is intended to assist a library user of any reference tool (whether print, electronic, online, or CD-ROM) to locate the monographic version if the library has purchased this version but not a subscription to the source journal.
- individual articles/chapters in any Haworth publication are also available through the Haworth Document Delivery Service (HDDS).

ABOUT THE EDITOR

Donald R. Koepke, MDiv, BCC, is the Director of the California Lutheran Homes Center for Spirituality and Aging, Anaheim, California. He earned his Master of Divinity from Lutheran School of Theology at Chicago and completed a year-long residency in Clinical Pastoral Care at the UCLA Medical Center in 1995. He also earned a Certificate in Gerontology at the Geriatric Pastoral Care Institute at the Center for Aging, Religion, and Spirituality, Minneapolis, Minnesota. Rev. Koepke is a member of the American Society on Aging, Forum on Spirituality and Religion, and serves on the Forum's Governing Council as well as the National Council on Aging's National Interfaith Coalition on Aging, serving as secretary to its Delegate Council. He is a Board Certified Member of the Association of Professional Chaplains and endorsed by the Evangelical Lutheran Church in America for Specialized Ministry. He has been a guest lecturer at the King-Drew Medical School; the California State University, Los Angeles Royball School for Applied Gerontology; the University of Texas, Pan American; Citrus College and Chaffey College and has consulted on Spiritual Caregiving with several multi-facility long-term care organizations. He is a board member of the Council on Aging of Orange County as well as South Bay Retirement Community and an Advisory Council member, Department of Gerontology, University of La Verne.

Pastor Koepke engages staff of long-term care communities with the belief that "Aging is a spiritual journey" and thus is worthy of respect, attention, and encouragement by staff of all disciplines. He has guided 50 congregations in southern California through a process called "Elder Ministry in the Congregation" whereby each congregation develops its own model for older adult ministry. This book is based upon his experiences with the Elder Ministry in the Congregation process.

Ministering to Older Adults: The Building Blocks

CONTENTS

About the Contributors

Donald R. Koepke, MDiv, BCC, has had extensive experience in both parish ministry and long-term care chaplaincy and is now the Director of the California Lutheran Homes Center for Spirituality and Aging. His headquarters is in Anaheim, California.

Bonnie Stover is currently Director of the Auxiliary of California Lutheran Homes and Director of Volunteer Services for Front Porch, a not-for-profit company serving seniors in California, Arizona, Louisiana, and Florida. She has worked in the field of volunteer management for over 20 years.

Rod Parrott, MDiv, MA, is Dean of the Disciples Seminary Foundation in Claremont (retired June 30, 2005). A member of the Ecumenical Network on Spirituality and Aging in Southern California, he has managed pastoral continuing education and lay leadership conferences on aging for the past decade.

Rev. Dr. Robert Carlson is Vice President of Episcopal Senior Ministries in Washington, D.C. and Immediate Past Chair of the National Interfaith Coalition on Aging. Prior to his retirement from full time ministry he served as a parish priest, Professor of Ministries at Seabury-Western Seminary and Canon for Clergy Deployment in Pennsylvania and in Washington, D.C.

Ray Mattes, MSG, MPA, MA, is a gerontologist, pastoral theologian, and administrator. He currently serves as Executive Director of the Collaborative Project for Aging Religious, Inc. which provides eldercare consultations, program development, retreats, and workshops on the topics aging, spirituality, and life enhancement to religious congregations.

Robert A. Rost, DMin, is Pastor of Nativity of Mary Catholic Church of Independence, MO and is also Director and a faculty member of the Center for Aging, Religion, and Spirituality (CARS).

Judy Armstrong Bever, MDiv, is Chaplain at NBA California Christian Home of Rosemead, CA and a frequent presenter and producer of workshops on aging for the Christian Church (Disciples of Christ) in Southern California.

James Ellor, DMin, PhD, is Associate Professor, School of Social Work, and Director of the Institute for Gerontological Studies at Baylor University. He is the Editor-in-Chief of the *Journal of Religion, Spirituality & Aging* of The Haworth Press, Inc. and the co-author of several books including *Enabling the Elderly: Religious Institutions Within the Community Service System,* and *Understanding Religious and Spiritual Aspects of Human Service Practice.*

Why Older Adult Ministry?

Donald R. Koepke, MDiv, BCC

SUMMARY. *Ministering to Older Adults: The Building Blocks* offers an approach to the systematic development of programs and services for the aged that focuses on spiritual not just psychosocial needs. This model has been proven to work in over forty congregations of various denominations in southern California. The questions surrounding the task of planning older adult ministries are explored without giving the answers, which must come from the reader. This chapter concludes with four reasons why a faith community should begin and/or enhance their older adult ministry in preparation for exploring the rest of the book. *[Article copies available for a fee from The Haworth Document Delivery Service: 1-800-HAWORTH. E-mail address: <docdelivery@haworthpress.com> Website: <http://www. HaworthPress.com> © 2005 by The Haworth Press, Inc. All rights reserved.]*

KEYWORDS. Systemic, spiritual, psychosocial, model, theology, tradition, experience, grey hair

Since the initiative of the current wave of older adult ministries in the 1970s, the most common approaches emphasize psychosocial support of older adults. These important programs address such issues as meaning in retirement. One such group was the *S. O. B.* Club. It was founded by a Presbyterian pastor who heard from the older women of his parish

---

[Haworth co-indexing entry note]: "Why Older Adult Ministry?" Koepke, Donald R. Co-published simultaneously in *Journal of Religion, Spirituality & Aging* (The Haworth Pastoral Press, an imprint of The Haworth Press, Inc.) Vol. 17, No. 3/4, 2005, pp. 1-6; and: *Ministering to Older Adults: The Building Blocks* (ed: Donald R. Koepke) The Haworth Pastoral Press, an imprint of The Haworth Press, Inc., 2005, pp. 1-6. Single or multiple copies of this article are available for a fee from The Haworth Document Delivery Service [1-800-HAWORTH, 9:00 a.m. - 5:00 p.m. (EST). E-mail address: docdelivery@haworthpress.com].

Available online at http://www.haworthpress.com/web/JRSA
doi:10.1300/J496v17n03_01

that there was a need for activities to engage newly retired men in order to *get them out from underfoot of their wives.* Many other groups have taken on holiday meals, support groups, and friendly visiting. More recently, congregations have begun to ask the question *"how do we focus our programs more holistically to include spirituality?"*

This volume is based upon the experience gleaned from teaching "Elder Ministry in the Congregation," a model for Older Adult Ministry Development. To date, forty congregations have experienced a planning process in which clusters of congregations meet together for planning one day per month for six-months. As a result: twenty-four of those congregations have, at present, an organized, intentional, and focused older adult ministry. Some congregations have been suburban churches, some city churches. A few were large–worshipping over four hundred persons per week. Some are smaller, with fewer than a hundred worshippers. Most have been moderate in size, worshipping between one hundred to two hundred persons per week. Most are multi-generational congregations but a few were inundated with gray hair. A few congregations have had paid staff specializing in Older Adult Ministries (OAM); however, most have only one pastor and an all-volunteer committee. This model of program development has worked across the board for those congregations that have trusted the process, done the homework, and have been intentional and focused in their planning.

This model does not advocate for a one-size-fits-all model of OAM. Instead, it will share a planning process in which the essential questions are raised, allowing for planning committees and the reader to develop answers that fit the needs, culture, history and structure of the congregation. The Appendix has camera-ready forms and charts to be used to guide the planning process.

WHY AN OLDER ADULT MINISTRY?

Why develop an older adult ministry in a congregation? Few congregations have such a ministry. Fewer still provided such ministry in the past. Why now?

First of all, the number of older adults in the United States and many other countries worldwide is increasing. The elderly have always been with us. In recent years, Ronald Reagan became the oldest person to be President of the United States. John Adams, 91 years old (1735-1826), was the previous holder of this distinction (John Adams was President of the United States from 1797-1801). Older adults are critical both as citizens in the community and as parishioners in the church. Seniors surpass all other age groups in voter turnout in most elections. They are also critical in congregations as leaders, role models, and as persons who contribute financially in disproportionate amounts.

In 1900, the average life span in the U.S. was forty-seven years. Today, life expectancy is seventy-seven years. The U.S. Census notes that in 1990, 1.2% of the population was over 85 (3 million) while just 10 years later, 1.5% of the U.S. was over 85 (4.3 million)[1] (U.S. Census Gov: General Demographic Characteristics). There is expectation that by the year 2050, 1.4 million persons in the U.S. will be age one hundred and over.

Yes, people are living longer. However, they are also living longer in their homes. Even the Federal and State Governments attempt to help persons remain in their homes as long as possible, developing programs such as Meals on Wheels, Care Connections, and Home Care. Today, persons usually enter a retirement community because they either need services or are anticipating needing services. Until that time, the elderly remain where they always have been: in their homes and in their congregations. If any church organization is going to address the needs of the elderly within a community it is going to be the congregation, not some agency of the church. There is more.

Eighty percent of all caregiving is done by relatives within the home, and the need for assistance with at least one "activity of daily living" (bathing, dressing, etc.) doubles every five years beyond age sixty-five.[2] ("Caregiving in the U.S.–A survey conducted by the National Alliance for Caregiving and AARP, April 2004," pp. 9-47). For example, in a group of one hundred persons age sixty-five, let us hypothetically suggest that five need caregiving assistance. By age seventy that same hundred people will have ten persons needing assistance. By age seventy- five the number will have grown to twenty. By age eighty, forty will need care. By age eighty-five, around eighty of the original one hundred will need some type of assistance in order to have quality of life. Couple this statistic with the previous one, where eighty per cent of all caregiving is done by relatives in the home and one quickly sees the challenge for congregations. No longer can we say "let our faith-based social service agency fill the need." The fact is that people are not calling the agency until they are forced to call. They remain in their homes, in the community, in the congregation.

Why Have Older Adult Ministries in a Christian Congregation?

There are essentially four reasons why Christian congregations should be at the forefront of providing services to and with older adults in their communities. Compassion for the aged is reflected in virtually all of the world's religions. For example, Christians live in the belief that they are loved by God. They are not loved because of what they can do or what they have done but because of God's love (as ultimately seen in Jesus on a cross). People of any age need to hear that they don't have to produce in order to be loved and worthy. For the elderly, the diminishments of age make that belief not just important to life but essential for life. To people who–for reasons outside their control–are unable to drive a car, balance a checkbook or see clearly enough to cook a meal, the words "you are loved just as you are" take on a life-giving meaning. That idea is often hard to accept but that is the reason for the ministry: to help people surrender in trust.

A second reason for older adult ministries in a Christian congregation is that many churches *affirm the value of tradition.* Many still celebrate the birthdays of saints who are 1,500 years old. The essential stories are familiar (like reading the story of Jesus' birth on Christmas Eve from the King James' Version). To people who are trying to make sense out of their lives and preserve their sense of self in a fast-changing world, where to be young is king, the affirmation that the past is valuable and worthy of reflection if not emulation, is a powerful word indeed.

Third, many Christian congregations (within their faith group) have *lots of practice* providing ministry to and with older persons. Many denominations have provided a ministry with older adults for centuries. Lutheran Social Services, Catholic Charities, Presbyterian Homes, and Methodist groups have provided the staples of life for thousands of people. In fact, the present day retirement community–even if it is not faith-based–owes its life to churches that first began this type of ministry in America.

However, the fourth reason is the best. Christian congregations should become involved in older adult ministry because within their membership *they have a lot of gray hair.* What do people say to each other around the coffeepot of many congregations that perhaps are dwindling in numbers? "What we need around here are more young people." Is that statement true? Is it but a caving in to American cultural worship of youth? Is it failing to reflect local demography? Older people often age in place creating what they perceive to be a problem with too many older adults and not enough young people. The challenge is to support older congregations to see the presence of older adults as a strength rather than a weakness.

In the past, churches were grown with young people. Many an elder can remember 250 children in a Sunday school or fifty people in the "newly married" group at church. The strategy seemed to be: "Get people to commit themselves while they are young and you will have an active church member for fifty years." However, is that paradigm still operative? For decades since World War II, America has been a country on the move. Talk with most people and much of their family lives more out-of-state than out-of-the-neighborhood. It is my understanding that the average stay in an American home is five years, not fifty . . . except for the elderly. Of course, sooner or later, older persons leave the community either to "live close to the kids" or to enter a retirement community. Still, their stay in the community is much longer.

For example, a congregation makes a concerted effort to reach out to older persons above sixty-five years of age. Not only are they reaching out to a group that few churches in the community even thinks about, but there are an increasing number of sixty-five-year-olds each year within their community. Where younger persons remain for an average of five years, persons age sixty-five are not only more healthy and active than the past but they might be in the community for fifteen years (seventy-seven being the average life span). In a presentation given on February 9, 2000, entitled "Aging in the 21st Century," Stephen Sapp said that if a congregation focused solely on older adults for their new members, providing a vital, focused ministry, that congregation would experience, on average, a five per cent to ten per cent net increase in membership. Stephen Sapp is Professor and Chair of the Department of Religious Studies, University of Miami. He is the author of several books including *Light on a Gray Area: American Public Policy on Aging,* Abington Press, 1992.[3]

One chaplain in a retirement community recently noted that many of the residents who are still able to worship in churches in the community are bored with their church. It's not that nothing is going on. It's just that nothing is going on for them. The sermons, hymns, and the style of worship are geared to younger folk. The church is still proclaiming a message but not one that answers the questions the elderly are asking. For example, many residents lament that they never hear sermons on death, or chronic illness, or suffering, all topics that are important to their lives. What they hear is child rearing, issues about the workplace, marriage, and personal development. It's not that they don't have those questions any more. It's just that there are others that are more pressing–questions raised by the very experience of growing older.

This text is meant to be a manual for the development of an effective, intentional, focused, older adult ministry in your congregation. It does not have lots of answers but raises a lot of questions for you, the reader, to answer.

The book is in three parts. "Part One: The Fundamentals," describes planning fundamentals such as:

1. Who are the Elderly? (Who is our audience?)
2. What do you wish your many programs to accomplish? (What is your mission?)
3. What skills and existing programs do you bring to the planning table that can provide a sure foundation for all that you do?

Only after these questions are answered are we ready to consider "Part Two: Programming Possibilities," and then conclude with "Part Three: Putting It All Together."

REFERENCES

1. The U.S. Census. General Demographic Characteristics.
2. National Alliance for Caregiving and AARP, April 2004, pp. 9-47. <www. caregiving.org>.
3. In a presentation given on February 9, 2000, entitled "Aging in the 21st Century."

PART ONE:
THE FUNDAMENTALS

Step One:
Who Are the Elderly?

Robert Carlson, MDiv

SUMMARY. An essential element in planning is knowing one's target group. Today, the description of the elderly in America has changed from a portrait of a frail person preparing to die to an active person who remains involved in life and community. Using statistics, the elderly are accurately described in terms of four categories: the Active, the Transitional, the Frail, and the Caregivers. Methods of discovering the elderly within a faith group are explored. *[Article copies available for a fee from The Haworth Document Delivery Service: 1-800-HAWORTH. E-mail address: <docdelivery@haworthpress.com> Website: <http://www.HaworthPress.com> © 2005 by The Haworth Press, Inc. All rights reserved.]*

KEYWORDS. Elderly, active, transitional, frail, caregivers, survey, focus groups

[Haworth co-indexing entry note]: "Step One: Who Are the Elderly?" Carlson, Robert. Co-published simultaneously in *Journal of Religion, Spirituality & Aging* (The Haworth Pastoral Press, an imprint of The Haworth Press, Inc.) Vol. 17, No. 3/4, 2005, pp. 7-17; and: *Ministering to Older Adults: The Building Blocks* (ed: Donald R. Koepke) The Haworth Pastoral Press, an imprint of The Haworth Press, Inc., 2005, pp. 7-17. Single or multiple copies of this article are available for a fee from The Haworth Document Delivery Service [1-800-HAWORTH, 9:00 a.m. - 5:00 p.m. (EST). E-mail address: docdelivery@haworthpress.com].

Available online at http://www.haworthpress.com/web/JRSA
2005 by The Haworth Press, Inc. All rights reserved.
doi:10.1300/J496v17n03_02

Who are the elderly? The answer could be very much like that of the legendary story out of ancient India of the four visually impaired researchers on the nature of the elephant. They concluded that the creature was like a tree, a wall, a rope, and a snake (Gaynor, 1999). The problem was not the visual impairment of the researchers but their failure to consider the whole picture. We see a similar failure in many popular notions of aging. For some, they are a bunch of rich old people living it up at the expense of the general economy. For others, they are a pitiful collection of depressed souls who have outlived their usefulness and are waiting to "pass on" in nursing home beds. For a few others, they represent a rich source of knowledge and experience waiting to be tapped. For others, they are a nuisance on the highways and a bother for their slowness in supermarket lines. For still others, they are the preservers of valued traditions and family stories.

As one of the elderly, I confess that I often get trapped in one perspective or another. In speaking to a family support group in a nursing home recently, I felt overwhelmed by the burden the residents were to their concerned families. Many of the patients were like my wife's aunt. She had known me for half a century but later, I was only a kind stranger who held her hand as we said the Lord's Prayer together. The fact that only five percent of the elderly are in nursing homes seemed hard to believe. I found myself living within a second perspective when my wife and I celebrated our fiftieth wedding anniversary with a river tour of Europe. We discovered that most of our shipmates were at least as old as we were and that we all did very well in climbing up to explore hilltop castles and in swing dancing in the ship's lounge after dinner. I experienced a third perspective a few weeks ago when I was invited to take part in a luncheon for thirty members of a congregation all over eighty years of age. Some of these octogenarians were there with walkers and wheelchairs, present only through the help of family members and parishioners, but most could make it on their own. Several were the same people whom I met earlier ushering at the door of the church and setting up the altar for communion. Who are the elderly? They are all of the above and more.

There have been many attempts over the years to delineate "stages of aging," often seeking to relate such stages to chronological age. A German glass beaker from the early sixteen hundreds pictured "stages of man" by decades from birth through the nineties and revealed the popular prejudices of the day. For the thirties, it simply said "A Man" but from there it was all downhill, ending with a picture of a decrepit 90-year-old and the words, "The Laughing Stock of Children." In the

United States, being "old" most often has been tied to the social security norm of sixty-five, a norm which may be going up as we adjust retirement age to the availability of social security funds. Older people themselves disagree about when it is they are "old." A study released in 2002 by the National Council on the Aging (Cutler, 2002, 17) found that fifty-one per cent of persons aged sixty-five to seventy-four considered themselves young (9 per cent) or middle aged (42 per cent), and only sixty-eight per cent of those over seventy-five considered themselves old or very old. Perhaps these results stem from the negative image of the elderly which prevails in our American society and causes us to resist thinking of ourselves as old. The one thing we can say with certainty, however, is that we cannot fit people into categories by their age. Some workers may be prepared to leave their desks or work benches at sixty-five or younger, but others resist doing so well up into their seventies and even their nineties. Some eighty-year-olds are homebound, while others spend their days delivering Meals on Wheels and helping their neighbors.

There are also considerable differences among the elderly as to the problems they and their peers are confronting. The same study of *American Perceptions of Aging in the 21st Century*, previously cited, inquired how serious older people regard the problems of health, crime, money and loneliness (Cutler, 2002, 5). Forty-two per cent reported health as a "serious" or "somewhat serious" problem. Crime was seen on the same levels by thirty-six per cent, money by thirty-six per cent and loneliness by twenty-one per cent. Surprisingly, when asked about how the same problems affected *other* older people, the percentages more than doubled. Despite these problems, the survey discovered that fifty per cent of their subjects sixty-five to seventy-four considered the present time "the best years of my life." Thirty-eight per cent of those from sixty-five to seventy-four said the same thing about their lives. Appendix A is a handout describing some of the statistics surrounding aging in the United States.

Remembering that we cannot describe older people by their chronological age, it is important to note that older people differ from one another and thus have different needs as well as gifts to offer. For convenience sake we can divide the elderly into four general categories: the active, transitional, and frail elderly as well as caregivers (which overlaps both the active and the transitional categories). Because of the sheer physical limitations of our bodies, any of us who live long enough will one day be in the frail category. At the usual retirement age, most of us, like my friends on the river tour, will be active, continuing to move about much as we did before retirement but enjoying more discretionary time to give to recreation or volunteer work. All four categories are growing in the United States because we are living longer, largely through advances in health care through medical breakthroughs and the accessibility of treatment because of Medicare and Medicaid.

THE ACTIVE ELDERLY

In terms of both needs and gifts, the active elderly are often indistinguishable from their middle-aged counterparts. They need a sense of belonging and meaning. They need spiritual nourishment. They need to be doing things which make a difference in their community and world. Because their time of life usually requires the transition from full time employment to retirement, they often need time and place to reflect on the losses that come with that transition and on ways to find replacements for the meaning and status that work gave to their lives. One congregation I know of has a group called "The Seekers" which meets weekly and attracts a variety of active elders to confront the issues of transition from work to retirement. While AARP has an excellent program on preparation for retirement, religious people also need to deal with the transition in its spiritual dimension.

The potential gifts of active older people to church and community cannot be overestimated. Too often the church taps its active seniors only for stuffing envelopes and setting up chairs for parish dinners, without regard to the wisdom and years of experience the seniors have. One congregation I know has recruited a seventy-three-year-old retired social worker to receive training in spiritual direction and to translate her years of doing therapy into being a spiritual guide for younger members. Fred, an eighty-year-old retired accountant, spends two days a week helping churches and nonprofit organizations in the community to computerize their financial records. Jane, a retired nurse practitioner, serves her small church as a volunteer parish nurse.

Clergy of a parish need to be involved in dealing with the gifts and needs of the active elderly in order to help make connections between needs and people and to enable lay people to exercise their ministries. A book by the late Paul Maves, *Older Volunteers in Church and Community*, contains a wealth of information on working with older volunteers. Maves points out that it is crucial for clergy and other leaders to know how to recruit, train, support, and, when necessary, dismiss volunteers.

The Transitional Elderly

Elderly in this stage of aging are beginning to feel the limits put on them by their aging bodies. They have at least one ADL (activities of daily life) limit. Their mobility may be decreased and they may even need help in getting to worship and other church functions. They may be reluctant to expose their limits and their need for assistance. They may come to our attention only when someone observes that they don't come to our meetings as often as they used to come. However, their needs to be in community and to serve persist, as well as possible need for transportation and home visits.

Elders in transition require a good deal of tactful attention. Their spiritual needs may include some thoughtful reflection on where they are in life, the so-called "life review" with a pastor or sensitive lay friend. Their needs for community may require the offer of a car pool and assurance that meeting places are accessible for persons using walkers or wheelchairs. Their need to be useful may be limited to services they can provide at home or elsewhere with transportation help.

The danger of the transitional stage of aging is that these parishioners may begin "getting lost" from the church and may get out of the habit of Sunday worship. One of the most useful services an active senior volunteer can provide is that of keeping track of older parishioners to help minimize the danger of their being lost due to their growing physical limits.

The Frail Elderly

Since the fastest growing segment of our population in the United States is that of people over eighty years of age, we may expect a similar growth in the number of frail elderly. They often need assistance with two or more activities of daily life. Some of the frail elderly are able, with help, to attend worship and other church functions but others are homebound or in extended care facilities. Five per cent of those over sixty-five are in the latter category.

One of the first questions I ask when I begin an interim ministry in a congregation is "Who are the homebound and nursing home residents in this congregation?" This information is especially important for a church in transition because it is in that period that many frail members can be lost. It is a tragedy for a church when members of the congregation who have worshiped and served faithfully for many years are forgotten and lost.

The frail elderly also have a need to belong and to serve. Service opportunities may seem very limited but there are things the frail elderly can do which are vital to a church's life. One such frail woman in a congregation I served was one of the most upbeat and spiritually positive people I have ever known. Elizabeth had a calling list of other homebound persons and her voice and positive witness was a daily treat to all on her list. She also had a long "to pray for" list and I felt supported every day by being one of the people on that list.

The needs of the frail elderly for community are often more difficult to satisfy. In a congregation of any size it may be hard for the pastor to get by more than once a month, but clergy are not the only ministers in a congregation. Lay people can stop by after worship to reach out and include home or nursing home bound elderly in the worship. In my church (Episcopal), lay Eucharistic ministers can be licensed to take communion to shut-ins directly from the altar after the parish Eucharist, thus making them weekly participants in the communion fellowship. Other churches can utilize lay people to provide fellowship, recordings of the service or shared Bible readings.

When frail elderly reside in extended care facilities, similar inclusion can be provided by lay visitors. It is also important to remember that nursing home residents who receive regular outside visitors have been found to receive better attention from the nursing home staff than those who do not receive such visits.

One category of the frail elderly that is of special note includes those who are mentally or psychologically impaired through Alzheimer's or similar diseases. It becomes easy for us to neglect them with the excuse "O well, Mrs. Smith doesn't know us or remember we called from one minute to the next." That may be true, but as religious people we put a value on our "Mrs. Smiths" that goes beyond their disabilities. Resources we have in serving them are our biblical, musical and liturgical materials. I remember sitting on the porch with my eighty-seven-year-old mother-in-law some years ago. She didn't know who I was, but while we sat there we began singing some old hymns. I was surprised to find that she remembered every word. When we were done she took my hand, smiled, and said "You're a nice man." It was one of the most touching compliments I ever received.

The Caregivers

Caregivers are those with a primary responsibility for someone (usually a spouse or other family member) who needs assistance in carrying out the usual life functions. They may be active elderly, transitional or younger family members. Since more couples are living into old age, the likelihood of a husband or wife becoming a caregiver for the other is greatly increased. We tend to think of women as the most likely ones to take on this role but men also may have to serve as caregivers. One eighty-five-year-old man who had never prepared a meal or even run a washing machine or vacuum cleaner suddenly had to adapt to the fact that his eighty-three-year-old wife would probably be bedridden for the rest of her life. He complained a lot to his two sons who lived half a continent away, but when they spoke to him about helping him place their mother in a suitable nursing home, he confessed that he could never do that. He needed to have their ear for complaining but as long as he could manage as caregiver he would do so. Another seventy-seven-year-old man has spent ten years being the primary caregiver for his wife with Parkinson's disease and has done so with great care and compassion.

Whether the caregiver is a man or a woman, however, the role can be very draining, both physically and emotionally. The caregiver often has little life of her or his own, and such simple things as doing the shopping or attending church services may require great effort and planning. The church can play an important role in ministering to the caregivers as well as to the frail person being served. Caregivers need respite assistance, whether it is for a few hours, a day, or a few days of needed vacation. Parish nurses can play an important part in training or backing up parishioners who offer respite for the caregiver, helping them to know what to do in case of an unlikely medical emergency. The caregiver also needs ministering to in terms of being included in the community life of the congregation; just having someone else to talk to can be a great gift to active caregivers who find themselves as homebound as their spouses.

Discovering Who the Elderly Are in Your Congregation

One truth that I cannot overemphasize is that the elderly cannot be lumped into one group or category by age. Each elder and the body of elders in each congregation are unique. We cannot begin an effective ministry with them without finding out who they are. How do we do this? The simple answer, of course, is that we do it by asking them, by asking the people we seek to serve and whose talents we wish to utilize.

Before asking older members what they need to give to and receive from the church, however, we need to do three things: (1) be clear with the clergy leadership what it is we are hoping to do and to enlist their co-operation, (2) enlist the help of a group of parishioners who have an interest in the enterprise and who are willing to follow through in study and action, and (3) find out what ministries with and to older persons are already in place.

In the years that I have been involved in ministry with and for older persons, I have found that not all clergy share my concern. Some years ago I was asked to meet with a group of seminary students on the topic of aging.[1] I began by citing the statistic from the Episcopal Church that in an average congregation, fifty-six percent of the members are over fifty and twenty-four percent are over sixty-five. The students reacted with alarm and proposed that we strengthen our efforts in youth ministry! While not wanting to slight our needs for youth ministry, the point I wished to make was that seminary students need to prepare themselves to deal with the needs of older adults. Unfortunately, we have seen this same reluctance to support a ministry with older adults on many of our national church levels where budgets have been cut or eliminated altogether. On the local church level, however, it is important that clergy leadership be sensitive to the needs and gifts of their older members if an intentional senior ministry is to go forward.

In advancing ministry with and to older adults, it is useful to have a group of parishioners who share a concern for this ministry and are willing to follow through to implement what they discover about the seniors in their midst. Older members, of course, should be part of this group.

We need to begin with an acknowledgment of what is already happening in the congregation. No congregation is totally without senior ministry. Seniors are part of the worshiping community and are likely to be key people in the work and ministry of the church. The clergy and lay leaders of the congregation can provide the basic information. Richard Gentzler, in his book *Older Adult Ministry*, provides a useful "Local Church Program Assessment Form" (73) which can help elicit information on who are the older people in this congregation. (See an adapted Church Program Assessment Form in Appendix D, page 176.) Appendix B has a tool that might help a planning committee discover "Who are the Elders" within a faith community.

The "experts" for answering the question of who are the elderly in a congregation, however, are the elderly themselves. Questionnaires can be of some value in securing information, though they are usually least helpful when sent out and returned in the mail and of more value when they are given in person with opportunity for dialog and feedback. A good example of a questionnaire can be found in the guide *Ministry with Older Adults in the Church*, published by the Evangelical Lutheran Church (Ellor et al., 2000, 18) or the assessment form found in Appendix F (page 183).

Another option for gathering information from elders themselves is to meet with a group, using a series of open-ended questions such as the following:

1. In what ways are you receiving ministry from this church? What helps that ministry to happen? What hinders it?
2. In what ways are you giving ministry/service as a member of the church? What helps you in giving it? What hinders it?
3. What needs do you have which the church might address?
4. What needs do you see other older people having which the church could address?
5. What gifts do you have which you would like to exercise through the church but are not now exercising? How might the church help you to exercise them?

The group leader needs to give sufficient time for thought and reflection so that new ideas can be generated and so that the less talkative members can have opportunity to express themselves. The responses should be recorded on newsprint so that they can be seen by everyone and so that they can be compiled and circulated to everyone.

One group we must not forget in asking the above questions is the frail elderly who are homebound or in nursing homes. They need to speak for themselves and be heard with the assurance that their requests to serve and be served will receive a response. A congregation must be prepared to follow through with its senior ministry, especially with its disabled members.

Who are the elderly? They are a large and growing part of all of our churches and our society. They are a varied group of people with varied gifts and needs. If a congregation fails to respond to those varied needs, it will fall short of our Lord's injunction to serve as of doing service to him. If a congregation fails to recognize and use the varied gifts for ministry and service in its older members, it will deprive itself of generations of wisdom and experience with which to enrich the church and its ministry.

NOTE

1. Understanding Episcopal Congregations Results from the 2000 Faith Communities Today Survey.

REFERENCES

Cutler, N. E., Whitelaw, N. A., & Beattie, B. L. (2002). *American Perceptions of Aging in the 21st Century.* Washington DC: National Council on the Aging.

Ellor, J., Kimble, M., & Seeber, J. (2000). *Ministry with Older Adults in the Church.* Chicago: Evangelical Lutheran Church in America Division of Congregational Ministry.

Gaynor, A. (1999). *Images of God.* St. Paul: Hazledon Press.

Gentzler, R. H. (1999). *Older Adult Ministry.* Nashville: Discipleship Resources

Maves, P. B. (1981). *Older Volunteers in Church and Community.* Valley Forge: Judson Press.

RECOMMENDATIONS FOR READING

Address, R. F., & Person, H. E. (2003). *That you may live long: Caring for our aging parents, caring for ourselves.* New York: URJ Press.

Arn, W., & Arn, C. (1999). *Catch the age wave: A handbook for effective ministry with senior adults.* Kansas City: Beacon Hill Press.

Carlson, D. (1997). *Engaging in ministry with older adults.* Herndon: Alban Institute Publications.

Carroll, J. W., & Wade, C. R. (2002). *Bridging divided worlds: Generational cultures in congregations.* Indianapolis: Jossey-Bass Publishers.

Cole, T. (1993). *The Journey of life, a cultural history of aging in America.* New York: Cambridge University Press.

Cutler, N. E., Whitelaw, N. A., & Beattie, B. L. (2002). *American perceptions of aging in the 21st century.* Washington DC: National Council on the Aging.

Ellor, J., Kimble, M., & Seeber, J. (2000). *Ministry with older adults in the church.* Chicago: Evangelical Lutheran Church in America Division of Congregational Ministry.

Gentzler, R. H. (1999). *Older adult ministry.* Nashville: Discipleship Resources.

Gentzler, R., & Clingan, D. (1996). *Aging: God's challenge to church and synagogue.* Nashville: Discipleship Resources.

Johnson, R. P. (1995). *Caring for aging parents.* St. Louis: Concordia Publishing House.

Kimble, M., & McFadden, S. (2003). *Aging, spirituality, and religion: A handbook* (Vol. 2). Minneapolis: Fortress Press.

Kimble, M., McFadden, S., Ellor, J., & Seeber, J. (1995). *Aging, spirituality, and religion: A handbook* (Vol. 1). Minneapolis: Fortress Press.

Moberg, D. O. (Ed.). (2001). *Aging and spirituality: Spiritual dimensions of aging theory, research, practice, and policy.* Binghamton: The Haworth Press, Inc.

Richards, M. (1999). *Caregiving, church, and family together*. Louisville: Geneva Press.
Seeber, J. (1990). *Spiritual maturity in later years*. Binghamton: The Haworth Press, Inc.
Tickle, P. (1995). *Re-discovering the sacred: Spirituality in America*. New York: Crossroad Publishing Company.
Tobin, S. S., Ellor, J. W., & Anderson-Ray, S. M. (1986). *Enabling the elderly*. Albany: State University of New York Press.

Step Two:
What Do You Want
the Older Adult Ministry Program
to Accomplish?

Donald R. Koepke, MDiv, BCC

SUMMARY. What is the purpose for an older adult ministry within a congregation? It is not a program but a process of spiritual care, spiritual development, and spiritual formation as older adults are confronted with challenges to their spiritual perspectives due to the changes inherent in the process of aging. The experience of aging is a teacher that can be denied only with great peril to the person. Various views of aging as a spiritual journey are shared. The support and guiding of the spiritual perspectives of older adults is the core purpose for an older adult ministry in a congregation. This central purpose must be overtly expressed through the writing of a mission statement for older adult ministry that will be a yardstick not only for evaluating present ministries but also for guiding their future efforts. A simple, easy-to-use method of developing a mission statement is shared. *[Article copies available for a fee from The Haworth Document Delivery Service: 1-800-HAWORTH. E-mail address: <docdelivery@ haworthpress.com> Website: <http://www.HaworthPress.com> © 2005 by TheHaworth Press, Inc. All rights reserved.]*

[Haworth co-indexing entry note]: "Step Two: What Do You Want the Older Adult Ministry Program to Accomplish?" Koepke, Donald R. Co-published simultaneously in *Journal of Religion, Spirituality & Aging* (The Haworth Pastoral Press, an imprint of The Haworth Press, Inc.) Vol. 17, No. 3/4, 2005, pp. 19-32; and: *Ministering to Older Adults: The Building Blocks* (ed: Donald R. Koepke) The Haworth Pastoral Press, an imprint of The Haworth Press, Inc., 2005, pp. 19-32. Single or multiple copies of this article are available for a fee from The Haworth Document Delivery Service [1-800-HAWORTH, 9:00 a.m. - 5:00 p.m. (EST). E-mail address: docdelivery@haworthpress.com].

Available online at http://www.haworthpress.com/web/JRSA
2005 by The Haworth Press, Inc. All rights reserved.
doi:10.1300/J496v17n03_03

KEYWORDS. Aging as a Spiritual Journey, spiritual development, mission statement, guiding principles

What is hoped to be accomplished by developing an older adult ministry? Is one goal to provide respite for caregivers? To organize telephone partners that can drive away loneliness, at least for a moment? To be a place for older persons to swap stories, or sing the old hymns that the new pastor hardly knows and seldom picks on a Sunday morning? All of these are wonderful goals, but what do you want those ministries to accomplish? If you could wave a magic wand and suddenly the ideal older adult ministry were in place, what difference would it make in the lives of the people within your community?

What is the reason for the congregation to offer an intentional, focused older adult ministry? The local senior center can provide out-of-town trips to local places of interest. It can probably do it better because it has the budget as well as the "critical masses" of persons attending the center.

The local senior center can provide meals and many do so with a hot lunch everyday at a moderate price.

The local senior center can provide a place to meet and greet, a place of fellowship possibly better than a congregation in that it may have the facilities, the exercise rooms, the card tables, the pool tables, the computers, and the large hall for group activities that foster interaction and fellowship.

However, there is one major thing that the senior center does not have (and probably will never have)–a desire to help people grow in their spiritual lives and perspectives–providing the tools, the experience, and expertise to aid them in that quest.

THE CENTRALITY OF THE SPIRITUAL JOURNEY

Ministry is a process, not a program. While vibrant, intentional programming is essential to an older adult ministry, the focus needs to be on the ministry, not the programming. Just because a congregation sponsors a gathering of older adults at a potluck, Bible study, or even through a caregiver support group does not necessarily mean that there is effective ministry taking place. Ministry is what is happening *inside* a person not what is happening on the outside. Programming provides the platform, the means, whereby ministry can take place. But the emphasis has to be on the goals and outcomes of the programming (what the programming produces), not on the programming itself. This perspective is essentially true with respect to an older adult ministry.

Aging is a spiritual journey. True, all of life is a spiritual journey, an attempt to make sense of the world and life within it. Yet with the coming of age, the journey becomes more acute, more obvious, less able to ignore or deny. It is often said that we live life moving forward but we reflect on life by looking back. The longer a person lives, the more there is to reflect on. For as we age we confront our humanity. We are confronted with the fact that we are not God, not the center of the universe, not in control of everything.

Take a few moments to complete "What does 'old' mean to you?" below. Answer the questions as quickly as possible, not stopping to think too much about your answer. If you are reading this book as a group, answer the questions and then take a few moments to share your answers with one another.

What does old mean to you?

1. When I think about growing old . . .
2. Growing old means getting . . .
3. Growing old makes me feel . . .
4. The older I become, the . . .
5. Older people never . . .
6. When I grow old I will lose . . .
7. Seeing an old person makes me . . .
8. A person can be considered old when . . .
9. When I am old I . . .
10. As I look back on the preceding statements, I feel aging is . . .

Name two things that you fear about growing older.

Name two things that you look forward to in growing older.

Comments on the Exercise

If you are like most people, many of your answers revolved around physical status. The ads say it well–"It's all right to grow old as long as you have your health," but what if a person loses her or his good health? What does that mean?

To Many, Loss of Health Means Loss of Self

Culturally and socially, to lose one's health is to lose everything. It means not being able to drive a car, walk to the store, or read the newspaper. That is why most people would envision the old Jewish birthday blessing "May you live to be 120!" as a curse, not a blessing. Think of the cartoon that depicts a physician saying to a very old, physically limited patient who is slumped over as he sits on the examination table, "Remember those extra years you added to your life through clean, healthy living? Well, these are them."

To lose one's health means that a person is on the brink of encountering that hated "D-word"–*dependence*–and if there is anything that is important a person, particularly to those living in the United States, it is the value of one's independence. To lose one's health and to become dependent is to lose one's value, importance, status. To be old, to be weaker, less capable, is to be sidelined by society and placed on a shelf and even ignored. I have heard many persons living in long-term care communities say something like, "Life is strange. The very time I finally have some of the answers to life, no one wants to listen" (Lee, 2005).

What the Judeo-Christian Scriptures Say

The Judeo-Christian Scriptures tell a different story. The Scriptures do not define the worth of the human being in terms of that person's ability to produce, to create or to be independent. The Scriptures define one's value in life in terms of relationship with God, a relationship that is first and foremost God-centered and God-directed, a relationship that is–*at its heart*–dependent: "We love because God first loved us" (1 John); "Come to me all who are weary and heavy-laden, and I will give you rest" (Matthew 11:28). One might say that the only action that God cannot forgive or deal with is arrogance . . . an "I can do it myself" stance that has no room for God (or anyone else for that matter). Jesus did not say, "Blessed are the independent" but "Blessed are the poor in spirit" (those who know their need for God), "for theirs is the kingdom of heaven." Jesus didn't say "Blessed are the strong, the capable, the one who is in charge" but "Blessed are the meek" (those who have their strength under God's control) "for they will inherit the earth."

What does it mean to age? Medical science can tell us what happens physically. In fact we in America define old age in physical, bodily terms. To a biologist, age is seen as a disease, something to fight and master. It is a function of the body characterized by decline, frailty, and death. Even the Bible acknowledges the obvious physical deterioration of older age (see Psalm 71 and Ecclesiastes 12).

Melvin Kimble, in a recent lecture, asked his audience the essential question, "I have worked so hard to grow old, is it worth the struggle?"[1] Some say "No" because the losses destroy any hope for a "quality of life." Others say "Yes," despite the obvious challenges that come with age. Yes, aging brings decline. Yes, aging brings loss. Yes, aging brings wrinkles. But aging also teaches us what we have always wanted and needed to know about life and living (Miller, 1995, 7).

Genesis 2 and 3

The Bible can point the way. According to Genesis 2, life is ideal. The man and the woman were connected. They could eat well. They even named the animals, showing power, influence and dominion. More than that, they were connected to each other. Genesis 2:25 states: "And the man and the woman were both naked and unashamed." Naked: open, receptive, intimate, without masks or games. Naked and unashamed: no guilt, no impulse to hide. Doesn't that sound ideal? But what made it ideal?

One answer is found in the third chapter. In the interchange with the serpent the woman is asked "Did God say that you should not eat of anything in the garden?" "No," the woman said, "we can eat anything in the garden except for the tree *that is in the midst of the garden, neither shall we touch it, lest we die.*" "You shall not die," the serpent responded. "Instead you will be like God, knowing good and evil."

The tree of the knowledge of good and evil was in the midst of the garden. It was right there, in the middle, where the man and the woman would pass it again and again. The tree did look great. The fruit was tasty. Eating from it could also make a person wise.

The point is this: what made life in Genesis 2 so idyllic was not that the man and the woman received everything that they wanted and desired. What made Genesis 2 idyllic was that the man and the woman accepted a "No" in their life. They accepted that even though they could do most things (eat of any tree in the garden) they could not do everything (eat of the one tree of the knowledge of good and evil). They embraced the fact that they were not God. Ernst Kurtz put it well, as to the human person "to be imperfect is to be perfect" (Kurtz, 1992, 63).

Age, the Teacher That Cannot Be Denied

Isn't that what age teaches us? And isn't that what we *don't* want to hear? Age confronts us with a "no" in life that we cannot ignore or deny. When we were younger we could just skirt around the "No" and emphasize what we could do. I cannot play the piano. I love music and would like to play the piano. Instead of playing the piano (which I cannot do), I sing. Thus my desire (need?) to create music is satisfied by singing. Someday I will reach the age when I may no longer be able to sing, but the scriptures say that I am more than my ability to sing. I am more than my ability to remember. I am more than my ability to be productive. I am a person. I am God's and God is the only thing in or out of this world that is going to last forever.

Age teaches me that truth-of-life–even if I don't want to hear it. I can close my ears to the message; it is called denial. I can become a grumpy old man and rail at my limitations. I can seek to ignore the fact that "I can't" by not acting my age and seeking to act younger. However, I can never escape the fact that I am not young, that I am certainly not God (which I am not) and never have been in control of my life.

Various Views on Aging as a Spiritual Journey

Jane Thibault points to that view as she speaks of aging as being a natural monastery (Thibault, 1999). What happens when a person enters a monastery? They leave "home" where they feel safe and connected and go to live somewhere else. He or she leaves home, which is his or her castle, to live in community rather than separately. He or she leaves a five-room house to live in one room. He or she lives in a place where there are lots to think about, to consider, to remember. Meals, medications, activities are on a schedule made by someone else. He or she is no longer king of the roost but instead must consider the needs of others as well as his own. This description certainly describes a lot of older people, especially those who choose to live in a long-term care community.

Kathleen Fischer points to this view as she speaks of our later years being an opportunity to turn inward and focus more on being than doing. "The task of spirituality is to convert the imaginations of both old and young to a new vision of the human" (Fisher, 1998, 15). Erik Erikson's famous "Eight Stages of Human Development" ends with "integrity," not "generativity," being the goal of life (Erikson, 1998, 56-57).

Age tells us that it is okay to fail–I can't walk up the stairs but have to take an elevator–something that was perhaps more difficult for me to accept when at age thirty-seven.

Age tells us that it is okay not to be in charge, as a person has to allow someone else to, using the words of Morrie Schwartz in the book *Tuesdays with Morrie*, "wipe my ass" (Albom, 1997, 22).

Age tells us to be grateful for life. Science fiction aside, we are mortal. The only alternative to aging is death, and while we can increase our longevity through better health-care, still the only way to live forever is to leave the mortal life–to die–to graduate as some say–to eternal life. For some (if not many), the greatest impediment to graceful aging is graceless denial of one's mortality.

Older People Crave a Place Where They Can Act Their Age

People crave a place where they can allow their age to speak to them. People crave a place where they can be themselves and not feel put down, ignored or marginalized. People crave a setting in which they can allow themselves to learn from the years of experiencing God in their lives. We, the church, need to and can provide that place.

So many ministries in the church are designed to fill time with busyness and provide a means for "fellowship." Both of these goals are fine, as far as they go but they are limited in scope and shallow in purpose. I would hope that all of what we DO in elder ministry is based upon WHO WE ARE as a people. I would challenge every older adult ministry to "hold their feet to the fire" (so to speak) and make every activity, service, and ministry an expression of who God has made us all to be.

Some of these intentional, focused activities will be invitational in nature–encouraging elders to look deeper and listen more, for we all tend to trust God's judgment more than God's grace.

Some of these activities will be educational in nature, encouraging elders to think more deeply and expand horizons.

Some of these activities will be service-oriented, encouraging elders to a sense of purpose by serving and seeing beyond themselves.

Of course, all events in an older-adult ministry need to be fun because laughing together is vital to life and exploring meaning together is crucial to real living.

What Age Teaches

Age brings opportunity and challenge. As the body slows, the spirit quickens because our vulnerabilities, our limitations are the doorway to God.

As the body slows, those who are willing to listen are treated to an experience of the heart as they recall God's grace past and anticipate God's grace future.

As the body becomes weaker, we realize that we are no longer in control and often discover that we never have been in control. For our bodies tell us in ways that we cannot ignore or deny what our heart has always perceived and faith has always known:

- That love is the greatest human need and God's greatest gift
- That God's love is unconditional and complete
- That God's love is broken on the cross and broken through bread and wine, just like the broken lives that we live
- That we are more than the sums of our parts
- That we are spiritual beings whose greatest challenge is to trust in someone who cannot be seen, touched, tasted, or felt but who can be deeply experienced.

Aging. Medical science sees the experience as a decline, a problem, and a disease, something to be conquered. Sociology sees aging as a series of losses and challenges of living. Psychology sees latter life as a time of memory-loss and depression. But we, who also love and respect science, sociology and psychology, know in our hearts and in our spirits that aging might just be God's greatest gift, a time of growing and surrendering to God's presence and learning to fall into his love.

Applying the Journey to OAM

What does all of this theology have to say about what we schedule in the older adult ministry of our congregation? It is simply this: Older Adult Ministry, like any ministry of the church, is not an end in itself. Older Adult Ministry seeks to accomplish something that is far greater than filling a calendar with lots of activities. Older adult ministry in the church ultimately seeks to be attentive to, tend to, cultivate, encourage, and deepen a person's spiritual life. If there is not a purpose, an older adult ministry (as any ministry) will atrophy and decline.

This purpose for ministry needs to be given voice so that its message is concrete, focused, forming. A mission statement offers an opportunity for planners to form a *common vision* of the tasks and goals. This common vision offers a light to guide future decision making. This voiced concept of ministry should be short, concise, and focused. It should provide a means whereby existing ministries can be evaluated and provide guidance for future efforts. Many people call statements of purpose "mission statements." Fed-Ex has a one-word mission statement, "Overnight," that evaluates and guides everything that they do and are. AARP has "Not to be served, but to serve" as its guide. Mission statements, according to Win and Charles Arn, should:

- Unify members of the group
- Give assurance that the group is doing God's work rather than just keeping busy
- Provide motivation for involvement and a basis for accountability
- Give the group overall direction
- Define what the group will and will not do
- Give a basis for measuring accomplishments (Arn, 1999, 63).

Hopes and Dreams as an Expression of Mission: Steps in Writing a Mission Statement

First of all, give yourself a moment to take a deep breath. Many people become intimidated when asked to write a mission statement, not knowing where to begin or how. Other persons have done so many statements that they are tired of participating in another futile task that, once completed, is never heard from again. So, take a deep breath. Don't make this too hard or complicated. Mission statements are simply an expression of our hopes and dreams. A camera-ready copy of this mission statement development form can be found in Appendix C (page 179).

Step One: List as Many Ministry Outcomes as You Can Think of in Five Minutes

Just let your mind flow. What are the desired outcomes of an older adult ministry within your congregation? Would you like people feeling closer to God? Would you like members not to be afraid of growing old? Would you like your friends to have information about available services that would enhance their later years? Again, do not put down specific program goals for your congregation, such as providing respite care or Bible Studies designed specifically for elders. At this point, focus is on what you would like any Older Adult Ministry (respite care, Bible Studies, telephone tree, etc.) to accomplish. How will you know that these ministries are doing what you desire for them to do?

Take a few moments to quietly pray for God's guidance and then jot down your desired outcomes (results) of an Older Adult Ministry in your congregation.

Step Two: Rank the Preceding Goals in Order of Importance

If you are a part of a planning committee, share your desired outcomes with one another. Note any duplicates. Look for creative thinking. All ideas are welcome. At this stage, none are discarded or judged.

Now, look at your list. How would you rank these outcomes in order of importance? If you are doing this exercise in a committee, this is a time for dialogue, for sharing why you believe a particular outcome should be number one and so forth. It is a time of listening to the heart of each other (or even to your own heart). What you are trying to do is to provide outcomes that will touch hearts, not merely fill seats or look good on a calendar. Seeking to give voice to such a high goal is both humbling and expanding. It is humbling because it requires an open heart and open ears. It is expanding because it challenges each person to grow beyond his or her personal perceptions of what should be the outcome of this ministry.

Step Three: Circle the Essential Words in Each Ministry Goal

This one is easy. In the list made in the preceding exercise, circle the essential words in each desired ministry outcome. You might even highlight phrases that jump out at you and/or touch your heart. This step will help you to crystallize and articulate the focus for each goal.

Step Four: Write and Refine a Mission Statement

Finally, based on the preceding steps, write a simple, declarative sentence that describes your hopes and dreams for your older adult ministry. Again, the best statements are short, focused, and self-explanatory. A statement that takes another document to interpret it probably won't be remembered or helpful. The process of "word-smithing" the statement can be time-consuming, but will be worth it in the end.

Examples of Mission Statements

First United Methodist Church in Fullerton, California, wrote that the "Elder Ministry Program is a ministry by, with and for older adults within and beyond the walls of our congregation. We shall continue to offer and deepen programs and services that will mediate the love and care of God. We shall endeavor to respond in new ways to the needs, hurts, and hopes of older adults in the community we serve."

Note the focus not on providing a ministry merely "to" older adults but "with" and "by" as well. Note also the desire to "deepen programs and services" (deepen is a very spiritual word) that "will mediate the love and care of God" not just make older adults feel better or have more fun. Note also the emphasis on responding in "new ways" which could be an answer to the words "We never did it that way before." Note also that the ministry will serve the entire community, both inside and beyond the walls of the congregation.

Messiah Lutheran Church of Yorba Linda, California, developed both a vision and a mission statement. "The VISION of elder ministry at Messiah Lutheran Church is to recognize and utilize God's gift of wisdom, age and grace to provide purpose, personal vision, and fellowship among the older members of our congregation and community." Growing out of that vision statement, "The MISSION of elder ministry at Messiah Lutheran Church is to identify and respond to the gifts, talents and needs of our older members in order to encourage spiritual growth in the congregation."

These statements also have some worthy parts. Messiah Church sees ministry as one of recognizing and using the gifts that God has already placed in their midst through the older members of the congregation. Also they believe that by so doing they will encourage spiritual growth in the entire congregation and not just with the older adults!

First United Methodist Church of Chula Vista, California, was more precise. "The Mission for Senior Ministry at FUMC Chula Vista is to bring all seniors into the community of the church, share the stories and nurture the spirit of each person to make Christ's love visible for all." This congregation sees that the task of older adult ministries is to listen to and encourage (share the stories) older adults, as well as to nurture their "spirit," two noble tasks to be sure.

Some Older Adult Ministries simply adopt the mission statement of the congregation (if it has one). That works fine as long as there is an accompanying statement that gives direct guidance to the OAM noting how the needs of older adults can be met by the congregation's statement.

St. Andrew Lutheran Church of Whittier, California, presented its congregation's statement: "We are a people of prayer and a Christ-centered, caring community of the one Christian Church. The Holy Spirit leads us to be Bible-based, life-long learners, faithful witnesses, and world servants for Christ. We joyfully share the grace and the gifts of God with all people." They then made a logo that depicted a group of people standing before the cross. In each quadrant of the cross was one of the four mission goals: People of Prayer, Life-Long Learners, Faithful Witnesses, and World Servants for Christ. The logo appears on most documents of the church. Growing out of this congregational statement is one for older adult ministry: "We will enable our elderly members to participate fully and age-with-dignity by meeting their unique needs through the use of the resources of St. Andrew Lutheran Church and the community."

St. Andrew Lutheran Church in Van Nuys, California, also made its OAM statement flow from its congregational statement. The statement is very spiritually focused. The congregation's stated mission is "to proclaim the Gospel of Jesus Christ so that others can experience God's unconditional love; to encourage all people to explore their spiritual relationship with God; to empower others through God's grace so that they can embrace life's crises, challenges, and opportunities with confidence." The Older Adult Ministry's goal is "To focus on spirituality, challenges and needs of the aging in our congregation; to explore opportunities and develop relationships with each other; to reach out to others in the community."

Where Are You in Your Planning So Far?

So far you have answered the essential question, "Who are the Elderly?" Without a simple, concrete, focused answer, any ministry with older adults will diffuse and be ineffective even if it is driven by good intentions. Who are the Elderly? What are their strengths and needs? If nothing else, your planning committee needs to agree on a vision as it relates to this population.

You have also thought about the central fact that aging is a spiritual journey and have wrestled with how to give voice to that journey in the form of a mission statement so that present efforts might be evaluated (and thus affirmed, changed, or discarded) and give guidance to future ministries.

You and your congregation do not come to the OAM table empty-handed. Even if your congregation has no OAM in place (which is highly unlikely) what strengths and skills do you possess that can produce a vital ministry? Answering questions such as the preceding is the purpose of the next chapter "Step Three: Assessing Readiness for OAM."

NOTE

1. Mel Kimble as expressed in a presentation made at Carlsbad by the Sea Retirement Community in Carlsbad, California, on September 26, 2004.

REFERENCES

Alborn, M. (1997). *Tuesdays with Morrie.* New York: Doubleday.
Arn, W., & Arn, C. (1999). *Catch the age wave: A handbook for effective ministry with senior adults.* Kansas City: Beacon Hill Press.
Erikson, E. (1998). *The life cycle completed.* New York: Norton Paperback
Fischer, K. (1998). *Winter grace.* Nashville: Upper Room Press.
Kurtz, E., & Ketcham, K. (1992). *The spirituality of imperfection.* New York: Bantam Trade Paperback.
Lee, V. (1995). *Pardon my planet: Omigawd! I've become my mother.* Kansas City: Andrews McMeel Publishing.
Miller, J. (1995). *Autumn wisdom: Finding meaning in life's later years.* Minneapolis: Augsburg Press.
Thibault, J. M. (1999). Aging is a natural monastery. *Spirituality and Aging, 11*(3).

RECOMMENDED READINGS

Alborn, M. (1997). *Tuesdays with Morrie.* New York: Doubleday.
Arn, W., & Arn, C. (1999). *Catch the age wave: A handbook for effective ministry with senior adults.* Kansas City: Beacon Hill Press.
Bell, V., & Troxel, D. (2002). *The best friends approach to Alzheimer's care.* Baltimore: Health Professions Press.
Carroll, J. W., & Wade, C. R. (2002). *Bridging divided worlds: Generational cultures in congregations.* Indianapolis: Jossey-Bass Publishers.
Cole, T. (1993). *The journey of life, a cultural history of aging in America.* New York: Cambridge University Press.
Erikson, E. (1998). *The life cycle completed.* New York: Norton Paperback.

Fischer, K. (1998). *Winter grace.* Nashville: Upper Room Press.

Frankl, V. (1959). *Man's search for meaning.* New York: Simon and Shuster.

Kimble, M. A. (2000). *Viktor Frankl's contribution to spirituality and aging.* Binghamton: The Haworth Press, Inc.

Kurtz, E., & Ketcham, K. (1992). *The spirituality of imperfection.* New York: Bantam Trade Paperback.

Lee, V. (1995). *Pardon my planet: Omigawd! I've become my mother.* Kansas City: Andrews McMeel Publishing.

Miller, J. (1995). *Autumn wisdom: Finding meaning in life's later years.* Minneapolis: Augsburg Press.

Moberg, D. O. (Ed.). (2001). *Aging and spirituality: Spiritual dimensions of aging theory, research, practice, and policy.* Binghamton: The Haworth Press, Inc.

Moody, H., & Carroll, D. (1997). *The five stages of the soul.* New York: Anchor Books.

Moore, T. (1992). *Care of the soul.* New York: Harper Collins Books.

Thibault, J. M. (1999). Aging is a natural monastery. *Spirituality and Aging, 11*(3).

Thibault, J. M. (1993). *A deepening love affair, the gift of God in later life.* Nashville: Upper Room Press.

Topper, C. (2003). *Spirituality in pastoral counseling and the community helping professions.* Binghamton: The Haworth Press, Inc.

Step Three:
Assessing Readiness for OAM
(Older Adult Ministry)

Donald R. Koepke, MDiv, BCC

SUMMARY. Assessing existing programs as well as the readiness of the congregation to receive new programs in the area of older adult ministry is an essential building block. An assessment of existing ministries is essential to discovering what needs to be developed. At the same time, the strengths and challenges of a congregation to develop and maintain an expanded older adult ministry is also important to assess so that starting points can be identified and needs filled. Often, the secondary gain of any congregational assessment is the ability to hear all of the voices within the congregation, help congregants to feel like they have participated in the process and to prepare them to expect something new. Tools for assessing existing programs as well as the readiness of the congregation are shared and explained. *[Article copies available for a fee from The Haworth Document Delivery Service: 1-800-HAWORTH. E-mail address: <docdelivery@haworthpress.com> Website: <http://www.HaworthPress.com> © 2005 by The Haworth Press, Inc. All rights reserved.]*

KEYWORDS. Assessment, existing programs, readiness, infrastructure

---

[Haworth co-indexing entry note]: "Step Three: Assessing Readiness for OAM (Older Adult Ministry)." Koepke, Donald R. Co-published simultaneously in *Journal of Religion, Spirituality & Aging* (The Haworth Pastoral Press, an imprint of The Haworth Press, Inc.) Vol. 17, No. 3/4, 2005 pp. 33-48; and: *Ministering to Older Adults: The Building Blocks* (ed: Donald R. Koepke) The Haworth Pastoral Press, an imprint of The Haworth Press, Inc., 2005, pp. 33-48. Single or multiple copies of this article are available for a fee from The Haworth Document8 Delivery Service [1-800-HAWORTH, 9:00 a.m. - 5:00 p.m. (EST). E-mail address: docdelivery@haworthpress.com].

Available online at http://www.haworthpress.com/web/JRSA
2005 by The Haworth Press, Inc. All rights reserved.
doi:10.1300/J496v17n03_04

During the twenty-seven years that I was a parish pastor, I discovered that many of the best ideas for ministry flopped. Perhaps many of the best ideas failed because the congregation did not do its homework. One of these pieces of homework is to understand who the recipients are for this ministry (Step One). Another homework item is defining what we wish our programming to accomplish no matter what programming might be selected (Step Two). Homework Task Number Three is to hear the voices of the congregation, not only in terms of understanding the needs but to assess the readiness of the congregation. Readiness in this case includes both the willingness to receive the ministry as well as to sustain it.

Assessing Readiness for older adult ministry takes two forms. First, it means assessing any existing programs. Second, it points us toward assessing the infrastructure of the congregation.

ASSESSING EXISTING PROGRAMS

Beginning an older adult ministry, or enhancing an existing one, does not happen in a vacuum. There are few congregations that are not providing some ministry that, although it might not be directly labeled as an older adult ministry, actually is. Appendix C (page 179) is a form for evaluating the existing outreach to older adults within your congregation. Take a few moments to fill out that form. If you are reading this book as a planning committee, share your answers with one another. Following are some clarifying comments regarding this assessment tool:

1. *What is the total membership of your congregation?*

   Count everyone. Many congregations are required to forward this statistic to their judicatory each year.

2. *How many persons in your congregation are in the following groups?*

   Active Elderly (raw number)_____ *percentage of total*_____

   Transitional (raw number)_____ *percentage of total*_____

   Frail "Elderly" (raw number)_____ *percentage of total*_____

   Caregivers (raw number)_____ *percentage of total*_____

Older adults are best categorized by these four groups based on physical functioning rather than chronological age. One person, age ninety-five, might be living in a nursing home while a different ninety-five-year-old is taking a trip to Tibet. Physical ability and, thus, accessibility is what is important here. Some congregations gather this information via a survey. A statistic that is 'close enough' can be secured by recruiting six older persons who know most of the congregation and having them decide, as a group, which category best fits each person. Such information should never be shared outside the planning committee (or perhaps this special task group of the planning committee) but it is crucial information for planning purposes.

3. *Who needs:* (raw numbers)

   *Transportation*_____*Extra Visitation*_____

   *Special Assistance*_____*Home-Centered*_____

Again, this information may be available through a ministry survey that is either locally developed or professionally administered.[1] It is also possible that same small task group above can speak from their knowledge of persons within the congregation.

4. *Do you have a social group especially for older adults? Yes/No*

   If yes, is it run by: Themselves_____Others_____

Whether an older adult group exists already is, of course, very important. However, it is also helpful to decide who runs the group: the older adults themselves, or someone else (staff person, person of younger generation, etc.)

5. *Do you have a group of volunteers to drive people to clinics, dentists, shopping, etc.? Yes/No*

   If yes, what is the age group of most of the volunteers_____

A simple yes or no is called for, but the follow-up question is of greater value in that volunteer opportunities are an important spiritual need for all older adults. If there is a ministry that helps drive seniors to places that they need to go, an expansion to include older adults as drivers could be important.

6. *Does your church have the following?*

Many congregations have ministries and physical facilities that are of great help for older adults. If any of the answers to this section is a "no," a follow-up question might be: "Why not?" Most of the items in this section are "easy winners" for a beginning or expanding older adult ministry.

a. *Tape recordings of church services for the home centered?*_____
b. *Ramp access to sanctuary*_____

Anytime that a place is inaccessible to anyone, there is a strong barrier for involvement in ministry.

c. *Ramp access to social hall*_____
d. *Ramp access to classrooms*_____
e. *Wheelchair accessible restrooms*_____

It might be expensive to remodel an older building, equipping it for full access, but it is vital to the success of any ministry with physically-challenged persons.

f. *Pull bars in restroom stalls*_____

This one is easy. A modest expense at a hardware store and some volunteer labor will make a powerful statement that all are welcome in your church building.

g. *Access to altar by wheelchairs/walkers*_____

It might be possible for a person in a pew to receive communion and pray but is that the best solution? Is there a way for persons in wheelchairs to get to the altar so that no one is made a "second-class" citizen? If there are stairs leading up to your altar, what about adding hand-rails? If desired, they can even be removable. One congregation in Covina, California, actually has a ramp on the side of their raised chancel allowing persons with physical abilities to not only commune with the rest of the congregation but also to serve as a worship leader.

h. *Bright lighting in sanctuary/social hall*_____

Dim lighting might be aesthetically pleasant to the eye but it does not make participation of persons with eye-sight problems able to participate in worship or social activities.

i. *Blank wall in back of altar/pulpit*_____

Again, persons with eye-sight problems (such as macular degeneration) cannot look directly at a bright window. First, all they see is shadows. More importantly, their eyes get tired or even hurt. Are there members who, as they get older, simply stop coming for no apparent reason? Do you see persons wearing sunglasses in church?

j. *Hearing assistance equipment*_____

Today there is no excuse for persons not being able to hear in a church. Small hearing devices that are very unobtrusive are available whereby wearers are able to sit wherever they wish and have the worship leader "speaking right into their ear."

k. *Place for wheelchairs prominently in sanctuary*_____

Some churches take out their back pews in order for persons with wheelchairs to sit. The concern is commendable, but what about shortening a number of pews throughout the church so that persons in wheelchairs can sit not only where they wish but also sit next to a friend or spouse who might not be in a wheelchair.

l. *Worship materials in large print*_____

In these technologically sophisticated days, larger fonts are always available. This can be especially important if your congregation projects the words to worship songs, etc., on a large screen since projected words can be more difficult to see than a "hardcopy." Raise your awareness of the challenge that some people might have in worshipping or socializing within your church.

m. *Meals on Wheels*_____

Items "m" through "y" are specific programs that many congregations have in place that provide a vital service and ministry with older adults.

n. *Home Repair Services*_____
o. *Home Chore Service*_____
p. *Parish Nurse Program*_____
q. *Stephen's Ministry (or similar)*_____
r. *Exercise/Aerobics Classes for Older Adults*_____
s. *Cooking and Nutrition Classes for Older Adults*_____
t. *Respite Care Relievers Program*_____
u. *Telephone Reassurance Program*____
v. *Adult Day Care Center*_____
w. *Prayer/Concern Chains*_____
x. *Emergency Hot-Line*_____
y. *Support Groups*_____List:_____
z. *Older Adult Service Recognition Program*_____

Some congregations have an annual recognition of Older Adults Sunday. It can be a time of affirmation and celebration not only for what they have been to the congregation in their more active days but for who they are as persons. Why wait until the funeral to express our appreciation for each unique life?

7. *Approximately how many older adults are doing volunteer work in your church?_____Total hours per week____ month____ year_____*

The Scriptures declare that my relationship with God is not complete until I have one hand in the hand of God and a second hand in the hand of my neighbor. The great commandment is to "Love God" while the second is to "Love one's neighbor." To be asked and affirmed as having a vital personal ministry outside of myself meets a deep spiritual need, no matter what my chronological age might be.

8. *Do the groups in your congregation organize trips, movies, parties, or other events for older adults? Describe.*
9. *Describe how your church minister to the needs of persons in your community who are not church members or attendees.*

It is not enough to say "Well, the ministry is here if people outside the congregation are wishing to participate." This question asks for intentional, sustained ministry to persons who are a part of our "extended community" (Arn, 2003, 105).

10. *Do you have volunteers who visit older persons in the hospital____homes____nursing homes_____*
11. *Are older adults represented on the governing board of your church or other committees of your church?_____*
12. *Does your church offer classes/seminars for older adults in any of the following: These ministries may be staffed by community organizations with whom the congregation collaborates.*

   a. *Grief and loss_____*
   b. *Spiritual development_____*
   c. *Death and dying_____*
   d. *Marriage communication_____*
   e. *Retirement planning_____*
   f. *Caregiving_____*
   g. *How to choose a retirement community/nursing home_____*

13. *Do older adults participate in the following ministries?*

Again, being involved in a ministry beyond the self is an essential spiritual need.

   a. *Local church teaching ministries?*

      For children_____

      For youth_____

      For young adults_____

      For middle aged_____

      For older adults_____

   b. *After-school Latchkey Programs for Children_____*
   c. *Preschool volunteer or employee_____*
   d. *Telephone Reassurance Program_____*

e. *Serve in worship areas:*

- *Ushers_____*
- *Greeters_____*
- *Lay assistants (liturgists)_____*
- *Readers_____*
- *Choir_____*
- *Song leader_____*
- *Soloists_____*

f. *Church office assistance:*

- *Bulletins/worship materials_____*
- *Newsletters_____*
- *Directories_____*
- *Mailings_____*
- *Receptionist_____*
- *Volunteer (or paid) office assistant_____*

14. *What programs, groups, or events are specifically intended to enhance the spiritual needs of seniors in the congregation?*

Spiritual growth may be defined differently in the various faith groups. However, such things as prayer groups, Bible studies, film and media discussion groups, private meditation, and prayer are often important to everyone in the congregation as well as the older adult. Sometimes, it is helpful to tailor these activities specifically for seniors; sometimes, it is preferable to make them congregational events. In any case, congregations should be clear that these are critical to the well-being of older adults.

Learning from the Existing Ministry Assessment Tool

Look over the results of your congregational assessment. You might be surprised at the number and the effectiveness of the ministries with older adults that are already happening. Focus on what is being accomplished rather than only on what could be done. Celebrate what you are already doing and save the results of the assessment for a future planning step. Identify any "quick winners" that may make a statement that older adults are welcome and valued within your congregation. Some of these "quick winners" would be to install grab bars in restroom stalls, provide worship materials in larger print, or provide tape recordings of Sunday worship.

Assessing Infrastructure

Assessing existing programs is only part of the story. What is the readiness of your congregation to support new ministries? If your existing ministries were doing everything that you wished, you probably wouldn't be reading this book. Because ministry is a process and not only a program, there is always more to assess.

Appendix D (page 180) contains a second assessment tool. This tool seeks to assess things that might be less tangible than a program. This tool is designed to assess the readiness of your congregation for the task of enhancing and building upon what you are already doing. Take the time individually to complete the Infrastructure Assessment tool. If you are reading this text with others, share your results. Seek consensus on each of the items.

Using the Assessment Tool

First, you are asked to rank your congregation on a one-to-five scale, five being best. No congregation is all ones and no congregation is all fives. In most categories, congregations fall somewhere in between one and five so avoid taking the easy way out by making a quick, superficial assessment. Many congregational planning committees that do not have an older adult ministry are too quick to say "Not Yet" and ignore congregational strengths that position them for an effective Older Adult Ministry (OAM) even if one is not in place at the time.

Second, you are asked to note why you chose this evaluation. The simple sentence or phrase that you write down might be the most important part of this exercise so that your evaluation is not 'just numbers' with no meaning behind them.

Third, an evaluation is not helpful unless there is consideration of the way the item explored can be improved. We all want to be a part of the solution and not just a person that complains without suggestions. Below, for further clarification, are some comments on each section.

Infrastructure Assessment Tool: Comments on Each Item

1. *Our program is intentional, planned, and focused*

Real ministry, real change in a person's life, real growth does not just happen spontaneously, at least not consistently.

Is your OAM intentional in that you have specific ministry goals that you are trying to accomplish? Without conscious goals, your ministry can be like a ship without a rudder, going places but who knows where?

Is your OAM planned? Again, effective ministry doesn't just happen. Effective ministry seeks to address the needs and perspectives of older adults, and thus careful and prayerful planning is essential. Even Jesus planned to ride into Jerusalem on a donkey and organized the disciples to provide for it.

Is your OAM focused (no more than two of the four ministry groups, active, transitional, frail, or caregivers)? If not, your ministry might be so diverse that it loses its creative force.

2. *Our program has strong roots*

The most successful older adult ministries grow out of present experiences and use tried and true resources. The alternative is to listen to the lament "but we never did it that way before." While any expansion or development might evoke such a response, the way will be easier if the program does not seem like it "comes from Mars" but rather is an outgrowth of existing ministry.

A Presbyterian congregation in Wildomar, California, is seeking to expand a highly successful, intergenerational drama program into a growth opportunity for all participants, many, if not most, of whom would fall into our understanding of elderly.

Bible studies can be "tweaked" and also become opportunities to talk about methods to communicate with persons with a dementia.

A Lutheran Congregation in Van Nuys, California, utilizing the resources of retired professors at USC, developed a lecture series on aging issues.

3. *Our program is based on demonstrated needs*

Everyone believes that he knows at least some of the needs of the older adults within one's congregation and community. The challenge is: Are these beliefs based upon fact or perception? While perception can be helpful, demonstrated needs are more tangible and helpful for planning. The demonstration of needs is crucial if a planning committee is to reach a consensus as to what the needs of the elders in congregation and community actually are.

A company called "Elder Resources" assists congregations in administering a 154-question survey to its membership. The survey results in a sixty-five-page document outlining the expressed needs of the congregation, from who is struggling with spiritual doubt to who needs help cutting toenails (a real problem for many older adults). Information about this inventory can be secured from the following address:

Church Resources
16835 Algonquin Street, Suite 231
Huntington Beach, CA 92649-3852

While it might be preferable, a congregation does not need to participate in a large program to survey its older adult membership in order to identify needs. The local Area Agency on Aging will probably have statistics regarding the elderly within your county. Many communities, especially those who sponsor a Senior Center, have often completed a needs survey in order to guide their staffs. Telephone interviews can be conducted by volunteers. Many of the interviews can happen using existing congregational groupings such as a choir or Sunday school class to reach respondents.

4. *Our program is enhanced by good record keeping*

Keep only as many records as you need for ministry planning. Do you really need to know the exact number of persons present at a given activity? If so, count them but use the information gained for its intended use. Do you need to know how many people are in the hospital at any given moment? In nursing homes? Living with family? How many caregivers do you have and who is visiting them, how often, for what reason? And, of course, what about finances? While most OAMs do not need lots of money to support them (unless there is the need for paid staff) good financial records are a must.

5. *Our program has identifiable leadership*

To whom does a member speak regarding upcoming OAM events? To whom can I speak if I wish to volunteer? How are these leaders selected? How do older adults feel about the process of choosing leaders? It is to be hoped that, those who are reading this book will become some of the identified leaders of your congregation's OAM.

6. *Our program has leaders trained in gerontology*

This is a big one. In the not-so-distant past, those clergy who were "not able to make it in the parish" could always become chaplains–especially to the elderly–but such is not the case today. With the number of older adults in our communities, the breadth of need that they express, the complexity of ministry to an age group that by definition is more individual than ever (everyone has had many years of experience to develop individual tastes, values, and behaviors), ministry to older adults is far from simple. Contact your local church judicatory or Area Agency on Aging for possible training sites in your area. Note the bibliography following each chapter of this book. Immerse yourself in the literature of aging. It will give you foundation, direction, and confidence. The Center for Spirituality and Ethics in Aging in Anaheim, California has a free, monthly e-mail newsletter called "CSA Spirit for Congregations." You may receive a sample copy by contacting <dkoepke@frontporch. net>.

7. *Our program has the support of the church council*

No ministry in a congregation exists independent from the whole. How has your church council been appraised regarding interest in older adult ministry? Remember, everyone approaches OAM from a perspective that has been shaped by cultural and not just Biblical understandings of growing old. There is a lot of "ageism" in American culture and thus the support of the organizing group (council, session, deaconate, vestry, etc.) is crucial for the success of an OAM in the long haul. It is very limiting to a ministry if that ministry is based upon the vision and effort of a few, rather than the support and counsel of many.

8. *Our program communicates well with the congregation*

In general, how effective is your congregation in communicating with its members? Does everyone have at least the opportunity of being exposed to all the information needed to make a prayerful decision regarding participation? Does the real information come through informal means and if so, are those informal channels effective? What methods of communication does your congregation have? Which ones seem to work the best? Was there a congregational event in the not-so-distant past that had successful and effective communications? What was done? What was learned?

9. *Our program communicates well with the community*

This one is hard and is often the most difficult for congregations. We have the ready ability to communicate with the congregational member-ship. Members open mail from the church. Community members, who may or may not know anything about your congregation, might tend to throw mail from your church into the circular file without opening it.

How goes your communication with your community? If your con-gregation were to have an event of intense community interest, how would you make your community neighbors knowledgeable about the event? What "tools" would you use? Are there any financial resources needed in order to communicate with community effectively? An older adult ministry is not something which one can, as they say in the movie *Field of Dreams*, "build it and they will come." It takes communication, even marketing and lots of it, to break through hurried lives and old prejudices with information. This is true even about good things that would be truly life-giving and helpful to community members.

10. *Our program is supported by a strong physical infrastructure*

The physical infrastructure is your facility. Many of the items regard-ing infrastructure are listed in the Local Congregational Assessment noted earlier in this chapter. Perhaps consulting the answers to many of the questions regarding lighting, sound, and access noted in that assess-ment might help in answering this section accurately.

11. *Our program has adequate financial and volunteer support*

While I am convinced that older adult ministry is person-to-person and thus does not need a lot of money for success, the access to capital is important. There is nothing more limiting to a new ministry than having no money available as seed-money for marketing materials about a coming event or having to beg in order to buy a new written resource, like this book. Of course, if your congregation desires professional OAM staff, money is very important.

12. *Our program is blessed with community ties*

Congregations can become an island unto themselves. So often, congregations become so focused on the good things that they are doing that they don't have time to develop community ties. This lack hinders growth of ministry, particularly if the ministry is to include persons from outside the congregation. Representation on inter-faith councils, connections with city government, involvement in the local senior center are a few examples of community ties that can be helpful in publicizing an older adult ministry, and may even assist in staffing programming.

In one congregation, the site of the local food program was "lost" for over a year as the old senior center was razed in order to make room for a new one. Because of our relationships within the community, that daily congregate food program, which provided hot dinners at a very low cost to older adults, moved into the church's facilities until the new site was available. What an enhancement of our older adult ministry that was!

13. *Our program is based on neighborliness and inter-congregational cooperation*

Congregations tend to become "lone wolves" with regard to other congregations in the area. However, cooperation–particularly when it comes to older adult ministry–can be of benefit to everyone. For example, four members of your church want to go on a two-day, one-night retreat focused in identifying the spiritual questions that arise in the latter years. The required number of participants might be hard to come by if only one congregation sponsored the event. If three come from one congregation, five from another, one from a third and ten from a different congregation, suddenly there are eighteen persons participating!

14. *Our program intentionally addresses the spiritual needs of the people who are served*

I saved the most important for last so it will stick in your memories. Older adult ministries in congregations are successful because they touch people's lives. They are expressive of the gospel. They are supportive of community, and *they intentionally tend to the spiritual needs of people*. Aging is a spiritual journey that has physiological, psychological, and social aspects. Aging is essentially a journey within, a journey of the heart, a getting in touch with how God has formed and shaped us in the past and continues to form and shape us in the present. Everything that we do, no matter what the program, should have spiritual development and formation as its central goal (see Step Two).

Some Questions to Discuss

Together take some time to review your evaluations. Here are some questions to ask:

- How might your committee insure that the OAM is intentional, planned, and focused?
- What might be done so that the program will have a sense of rooted-ness?
- What are the needs of your older adults? How do you know that your perceptions are valid?
- Are there opportunities in your area for training in gerontology that could be easily accessed to help in your planning?
- Is your organizing group (Church Council) on board?
- What can be done to improve communications about any Older Adult Ministry?
- Is sufficient thought and prayer going into program development so that the spiritual journeys of all may be affirmed and strengthened in every part of the ministry?

NOTE

1. Church Resources of Huntington Beach, CA has an extensive survey using the best in surveying techniques. Contact Cliff Pederson via e-mail: clif@elderministry. com

REFERENCES

Arn, C. (2003). *White unto harvest.* Monrovia: Institute for American Church Growth.

RECOMMENDED READINGS

Arn, C. (2003). *White unto harvest.* Monrovia: Institute for American Church Growth.
Arn, W., & Arn, C. (1999). *Catch the age wave: A handbook for effective ministry with senior adults.* Kansas City: Beacon Hill Press.

Carlson, D. (1997). *Engaging in ministry with older adults.* Herndon: Alban Institute Publications.

Carroll, J. W., & Wade, C. R. (2002). *Bridging divided worlds: Generational cultures in congregations.* Indianapolis: Jossey-Bass Publishers.

Gentzler, R., & Clingan, D. (1996). *Aging: God's challenge to church and synagogue.* Nashville: Discipleship Resources.

Kimble, M., & McFadden, S. (2003). *Aging, spirituality, and religion: A handbook* (Vol. 2). Minneapolis: Fortress Press.

Kimble, M., McFadden, S., Ellor, J., & Seeber, J. (1995). *Aging, spirituality, and religion: A handbook* (Vol. 1). Minneapolis: Fortress Press.

Richards, M. (1999). *Caregiving, church, and family together.* Louisville: Geneva Press.

Topper, C. (2003). *Spirituality in pastoral counseling and the community helping professions.* Binghamton: The Haworth Press, Inc.

Wimberly, A. S. (1997). *Honoring African American elders.* San Francisco: Jossey-Bass, Inc. Publishers.

Step Four:
Planning for Older Adult Ministry

Donald R. Koepke, MDiv, BCC

SUMMARY. Steps one, two, and three are now integrated into a planning tool for older adult ministry programming. Because of the diversity of older adults, a diversity of programming is required. A planning grid (tool) is described that can be used throughout the reading. This chapter forms an introduction to the whole of "Part Two: Programming Based on Spiritual Needs." The congregation's mission statement for older adult ministry is affirmed. A method of inserting existing ministries is described. Five aspects of older adult programming are identified noting how each is an expression of a basic human spiritual need. *[Article copies available for a fee from The Haworth Document Delivery Service: 1-800-HAWORTH. E-mail address: <docdelivery@haworthpress.com> Website: <http://www.HaworthPress.com> © 2005 by The Haworth Press, Inc. All rights reserved.]*

KEYWORDS. Spiritual development, lifelong learning, opportunities to serve, opportunities to be served, community building

---

[Haworth co-indexing entry note]: "Step Four: Planning for Older Adult Ministry." Koepke, Donald R. Co-published simultaneously in *Journal of Religion, Spirituality & Aging* (The Haworth Pastoral Press, an imprint of The Haworth Press, Inc.) Vol. 17, No. 3/4, 2005, pp. 49-54; and: *Ministering to Older Adults: The Building Blocks* (ed: Donald R. Koepke) The Haworth Pastoral Press, an imprint of The Haworth Press, Inc., 2005, pp. 49-54. Single or multiple copies of this article are available for a fee from The Haworth Document Delivery Service [1-800-HAWORTH, 9:00 a.m. - 5:00 p.m. (EST). E-mail address: docdelivery@haworthpress.com].

doi:10.1300/J496v17n03_05

OLDER ADULT MINISTRY IS MORE THAN A POTLUCK AND A BIBLE STUDY

Older Adult Ministry is more than a potluck and a Bible study. It might be helpful to explore five categories of Older Adult Ministry, even though they may never be seen in pure form. Adapted from a list first developed by Ramonia Lee (1989) the five categories are:

1. *Spiritual development*
2. *Continued education*
3. *Opportunities to serve*
4. *Opportunities to be served*
5. *Community building (social interaction) events.*

Each of these categories of ministry will be explored in depth in Part Two of this text.

The Centrality of Spiritual Development

Everything that a faith group does should be an expression of their spiritual values. Every action, every program that a faith group undertakes needs to have spiritual development as its goal. Jesus did not say to "Go into world and do social work." He said "Go into the world and make disciples." The parable of the separation of the sheep and the goats in Matthew 25 reminds us of the importance of clothing the naked and feeding the hungry. The sheep were seeking to love their God and one of the primary ways that a person loves God is by loving one's neighbor (1 John 4). The focus in loving God, serving God, growing more intimate with God, all of which is expressed in the words "growing spiritually," is found in both loving God as well as God's creation.

Thus the five categories (noted above) might symbolically "unpack" the phrase "Older Adult Ministry," but a faith group cannot forget their purpose: to love and serve God. Therefore Spiritual Formation is an essential method of spiritual development in older adults, but so is learning opportunities as participants expand their knowledge of God's universe. Thus, opportunities to serve are not merely an attempt to secure more volunteers for the grind of ministry but to provide a way in which people can get outside of their own needs, their own fears, their own limitations and "discover" closeness with God as they serve one another. By providing opportunities to be served, faith groups provide opportunities for people to express the interdependence that is human existence and is the doorway toward communion with God. Fellowship becomes community building, an essential expression of the spiritual life. Although a faith group might provide some programs that are similar to those at the local senior center, the desired result of each of those programs is different. Every action, every program, every effort is an attempt to increase intimacy with God.

A Program Planning Tool

The table presented here is a planning tool that has been helpful to many congregations (see also Appendix G, page 191). It is a matrix in which the five ministry categories noted above run across the top of the chart while the four ministry groups noted in Step One are listed down the side. These groups are: active elderly, transitional elderly, frail elderly, and caregivers. Refer to the "Assessing Existing Ministry" tool noted in Step Three. On the first page of that tool were listed the raw numbers and then the congregational percentage of older adults according to those four categories. Underneath the words "Active," "Transitional," "Frail," and "Caregivers," place both the raw number and the percentage of older adults whom you found to be in those categories. What is formed is a "grid" that begs for ministry opportunities (Part Two) to be listed according to both ministry category and ministry group (Step One) guided by a mission statement (Step Two).

Mission Statement

	Spiritual Development	Continued Education	Opportunities to Serve	Opportunities to be Served	Community Building
Active					
Transitional					
Frail					
Caregivers					

Your Mission Statement Is the Foundation

Write your mission statement (Step Two) along the top of the paper. Then choose programming (Part Two) that moves your congregation toward completing the purpose to which you have been called. Remember, Older Adult Ministry is a "process, not a program." A congregation does not have an effective OAM just because it fills up a calendar with events. It is only as older adults are affected by the program, challenged to grow and see life differently, that the ministry is effective. It is only as mission statements are used to evaluate and guide that a ministry, even if it has diverse parts, takes on a coherent whole.

Insert Existing Ministries onto the Grid

Refer to the Assessing Existing Ministry tool that was completed in the last chapter. Either with a pen of different color or by placing a large asterisk (*) in front of the item, categorize your existing OAM program according to the planning grid. Note that some items may not fit neatly into one category, so they can be listed in more than one place. List items according to the *intentional* goals of the ministry (what the ministry objectively accomplishes) not what you wish it would accomplish.

For example, an intentional visitation ministry to the frail, if it does not intentionally include time for prayer or encouragement regarding one's spiritual journey (see the first Spiritual Need in Part Two below), might be a service opportunity for active elders and also an opportunity to be served for the frail. However, even though an encounter between members of the church is ideally always a spiritual event, spiritual development is not the stated purpose of the visitation ministry and thus it cannot be listed under that category. While a workshop of caregiving skills might be a learning opportunity for caregivers as well as the frail and transitional, it is not spiritual development unless the spiritual side of caregiving is intentionally addressed. In the same way, while pot luck dinners might be a community-building event for the active, it would not be listed as a community building event for the transitional and the frail unless transportation was provided. Nor would it be an event for caregivers unless respite care was offered. Appendix H (page 192) shows how one congregation completed this step.

Learning from the Grid

Once all of your existing programs are listed, look at the grid again. What seems to be the present program emphasis? What ministry groups have received the most attention? Which ministry groups have been slighted? What categories of OAM have been strong within your congregation and which categories have been neglected? What areas are in need of support? These observations can go a long way toward effective program planning which will be completed in Part Three of this book.

Right now, however, you are ready to explore "Part Two: Programming Based on Spiritual Needs." As you read, jot down program ideas and thoughts in the appropriate places on the planning grid. This step will save you time in the final task, "Putting It All Together," which will be completed after you explore the five categories of Older Adult Ministry.

REFERENCE

Lee, R. (1989). From the Program Files of the Community Ministries Department of the Baptist Senior Adult Ministry. In dialogue with D. Koepke. Washington, DC: Unpublished.

RECOMMENDED READINGS

Bell, V., & Troxel, D. (2002). *The best friends approach to Alzheimer's care*. Baltimore: Health Professions Press.

Best, R. J., & Brunner, J. A. (1991). *Never forget our home, a healing guide for older people who choose to move forward to a new life*. Milwaukee: Montgomery Media, Inc.

Birren, J., & Cochran, K. (2001). *Telling the stories of life through guided autobiography groups*. Baltimore: Johns Hopkins Press.

Carlson, D. (1997). *Engaging in ministry with older adults*. Herndon: Alban Institute Publications.

Carroll, J. W., & Wade, C. R. (2002). *Bridging divided worlds: Generational cultures in congregations*. Indianapolis: Jossey-Bass Publishers.

Fischer, K. (1998). *Winter grace*. Nashville: Upper Room Press.

Gentzler, R., & Clingan, D. (1996). *Aging: God's challenge to church and synagogue*. Nashville: Discipleship Resources.

Kimble, M., & McFadden, S. (2003). *Aging, spirituality, and religion: A handbook* (Vol. 2). Minneapolis: Fortress Press.

Kimble, M., McFadden, S., Ellor, J., & Seeber, J. (1995). *Aging, spirituality, and religion: A handbook* (Vol. 1). Minneapolis: Fortress Press.

Koenig, H. G. (1994). *Aging and God: Spiritual pathways to mental health in midlife and later years*. Binghamton: The Haworth Press, Inc.

Koenig, H. G. (1997). *Is religion good for your health?* Binghamton: The Haworth Press, Inc.

Koenig, H. G., & Weaver, A. J. (1998). *Pastoral care of older adults*. Minneapolis: Fortress Press.

Lustbader, W. (1991). *Counting on kindness*. New York: The Free Press.

McBride, J. L. (1998). *Spiritual crisis: Surviving trauma to the soul*. Binghamton: The Haworth Press, Inc.

Miller, J. (1995). *Winter grief, summer grace: Returning to life after a loved one dies.* Minneapolis: Augsburg Press.

Moody, H., & Carroll, D. (1997). *The five stages of the soul.* New York: Anchor Books.

Morgan, R. (1996). *Remembering your story–A guide to spiritual autobiography.* Nashville: Upper Room Press.

Nuland, S. B. (1993). *How we die: Reflections on life's final chapter.* New York: Vintage Books.

Richards, M. (1999). *Caregiving, church, and family together.* Louisville: Geneva Press.

Rupp, J. (1998). *Praying our good-byes.* Notre Dame: Ave Maria Press.

Tobin, S. S., Ellor, J. W., & Anderson-Ray, S. M. (1986). *Enabling the elderly.* Albany: State University of New York Press.

Topper, C. (2003). *Spirituality in pastoral counseling and the community helping professions.* Binghamton: The Haworth Press, Inc.

Wallis, V. (1993). *Two old women, an Alaska legend of betrayal, courage, and survival.* Kenmore: Epicenter Press.

Wimberly, A. S. (1997). *Honoring African American elders.* San Francisco: Jossey-Bass, Inc. Publishers.

PART TWO:
PROGRAMMING BASED
ON SPIRITUAL NEEDS

Spiritual Need One:
Spiritual Development:
The Aging Process:
A Journey of Lifelong Spiritual Formation

Ray Mattes, MSG, MPA

SUMMARY. To grow old is but one chapter in a lifelong journey of spiritual formation. Spirituality can be defined most easily by what it is not. Aging is a process of discovery and pondering, reminiscing, and acting, integrating and meaning making, even surrendering to Life as it is, not as we will it to be. Spiritual insights are gained from James Fowler, Viktor Frankl, Thomas Merton, Paul Tournier, Adrian Van Kamm, and Rachel Remen. *[Article copies available for a fee from The Haworth Document Delivery Service: 1-800-HAWORTH. E-mail address: <docdelivery@haworthpress.com> Website: <http://www.HaworthPress.com> © 2005 by The Haworth Press, Inc. All rights reserved.]*

[Haworth co-indexing entry note]: "Spiritual Need One: Spiritual Development: The Aging Process: A Journey of Lifelong Spiritual Formation." Mattes, Ray. Co-published simultaneously in *Journal of Religion, Spirituality & Aging* (The Haworth Pastoral Press, an imprint of The Haworth Press, Inc.) Vol. 17, No. 3/4, 2005, pp. 55-72; and: *Ministering to Older Adults: The Building Blocks* (ed: Donald R. Koepke) The Haworth Pastoral Press, an imprint of The Haworth Press, Inc., 2005, pp. 55-72. Single or multiple copies of this article are available for a fee from The Haworth Document Delivery Service [1-800-HAWORTH, 9:00 a.m. - 5:00 p.m. (EST). E-mail address: docdelivery@haworthpress.com].

Available online at http://www.haworthpress.com/web/JRSA
2005 by The Haworth Press, Inc. All rights reserved.
doi:10.1300/J496v17n03_06

KEYWORDS. Spirituality, religion, inner growing, discovery, pondering, reminiscing, integrity, surrender, openness

In this chapter we will examine lifelong spiritual formation by identifying and exploring six formative tasks that impact the nature of spirituality and its development through the life course. As human beings, we are people who are shaped and formed by all the events, situations, and encounters of our lives. The years of one's life are a blessing, as they provide an opportunity for growth, development, and wisdom if one reflects on the very human and religious experiences one has had through life. Life is an ever-unfolding process upon which one moves through untold experiences and encounters that inevitably shape and form the individual. This continuous process of formation is fostered and supported by the individual as she/he openly embraces the ordinary circumstances life presents, through faithful listening to the voice within, and actively seeks to engage this openness as a means toward greater maturity and development. This is vital to our human growth. Formation then becomes a lifelong process as one is continuously impacted and changed as a result of the circumstances that one encounters through life. Formation encompasses and unfolds in all areas of one's life and as such is a process that invites continued growth and development of one's uniqueness and one's gifts and talents which evolve out of one's particular life circumstances. In so doing, this process of formation becomes a spiritual one as it calls us to explore who we truly are as individuals. In the words of Thomas Merton, "The spiritual life is first of all a life. It is not merely something to be known and studied it is to be lived" (Merton, 1993). In order for us to live the spiritual life, however, we must first establish a definition of it. In order to do this we will begin by exploring the question of "What is spirituality?"

The best way to define spirituality is to state what it is not. Spirituality is not a given doctrine, a belief system or a set of rituals. Spirituality is not about correct or incorrect answers, structured approaches to prayer or even holiness. Spirituality is about questions, searching, discerning, meaning making, and transcending. Spirituality is the essential element of who we are as human beings. Spirituality is that component of our humanness that draws us and pulls us out of ourselves in the recognition that there is something that lies beyond us. Spirituality is that force which motivates us and propels us forward whether we consciously realize it or not. It becomes a companion to the very human process of making meaning out of one's lived experiences thus enabling a person to have a greater awareness of the gifts one's life has bestowed, the values one holds, and the insight into one's own motivations. Spirituality is an integral part of being human and it becomes a formative process as it assists us in gaining a greater understanding of who we really are as a unique individual.

Psychologist Erik Erickson theorized that there were eight stages of human development beginning with infancy and ending in later life (Erikson, 1982). Each stage contained a specific set of tasks and corresponding virtue. For example, according to Erickson, in infancy an individual is confronted with the issues of trust vs. mistrust with the corresponding virtue being hope. If the infant receives loving support and encouragement, then the world in which the infant develops will be perceived as a trusting and nurturing place. Therefore the situations and events that the infant encounters during this stage of development will greatly impact the ways in which that individual ultimately perceives the self and others throughout the life course. The eight stages of human development according to Erickson's theory are: (1) Infancy–trust vs. mistrust; (2) Toddlerhood–autonomy vs. shame; (3) Childhood–Initiative vs. guilt; (4) School Age–industry vs. inferiority; (5) Adolescence–identity vs. role confusion; (6) Adulthood–intimacy vs. isolation; (7) Maturity–generativity vs. stagnation; (8) Later Life–integrity vs. despair.

Like Erickson, theologian James Fowler explored the notion of human development while focusing specifically on the ways in which individuals construct faith. Fowler theorized that human beings go through six stages of faith development. Each stage was associated with a specific period of human life. For example, Fowler stated that the first stage of faith development occurred in the childhood years which Fowler termed "intuitive-projective" faith as an individual took on the faith of one's parents and loved ones as one's own without distinction of one's personal uniqueness, etc. The sixth stage of development was that of "universalizing faith" which was described as a faith outlook that was both consistent and comfortable with the unanswerable questions of life since the emphasis rests solely on one's relationship with the transcendent. Fowler's six stages of faith development are: (1) Childhood–Intuitive–projective faith adopting the faith of one's parents; (2) School years–Mythic-Literal Faith associated with stories making personal what is heard; (3) Adolescence–Synthetic-Conventual faith–faith derived from the group one belongs to and conformity to the norms and views of the groups; (4) Mid-Life–Conjunctive faith–the process of making faith one's own by applying critical thinking and exploring the paradoxes which arise; (5) Mature–Open Faith demonstrated by one's ability to be comfortable with mystery and unanswered questions; and (6) Universalizing Faith–Deep consistent faith which recognizes that all is derived from one's intimate relationship with the transcendent (Fowler, 1995).

Adrian Van Kaam, CSSP, also studied the process of development and theorized that an individual's spiritual development was linked to specific dimensions that occur within the person's life that impact the way in which each individual is formed. According to Van Kaam's *Science of Formation*, each person is impacted by the *socio-historical dimension* that is made up of the culture in which we live, the point in history with its specific traditions. The second, *vital dimension* is that of our physiological and emotional structures and the ways in which these impact our responses to life. The third dimension or the *functional dimension* is the numerous ways in which an individual structures the activities and duties of life. It is the manner in which one creates order and discipline within one's daily routine whether that is through work, leisure or other responsibilities. The fourth dimension is termed the *transcendent dimension*; it is the manner in which one is in tune with the workings of God within one's daily life (Standish, 2001). The key to ongoing spiritual formation, according to Van Kaam, is the achievement of balance among all four of the dimensions. This balance creates consolation within the individual and enables one to more fully embrace the unique gifts of whom and what one has been called to become. In the words of author Parker J. Palmer, "Before you tell your life what you intend to do with it, listen for what it intends to do with you" (Palmer, 2000).

Exploring the depths of our own giftedness is the first step to getting in touch with our own spirituality. This occurs when we allow ourselves the permission and the time to look at our lives honestly and reflectively in a non-judgmental manner to "listen for what [life] intends." Our honest reflection occurs out of various aspects of our lives. It is found in the world that surrounds us, our painful experiences, our joys, the silence we allow our relationships, our own spiritual practices, and ourselves.

David Moberg, in his article *Spiritual Maturity and Wholeness in the Later Years*, notes that among all domains for change in human lives, the one that provides the most opportunity for continuing growth in the later years is the spiritual. The process of aging then contains such transformative elements by producing opportunities for deeper self-awareness, connectedness with our individual life stories, and the giftedness of the unique individuals we have become. The aging process can produce, but only if we freely choose to allow it to do so, a fertile place where things of the spirit can be explored more fully and a framework for the development of one's own spirituality is constructed in which the questions of our lives are pondered, explored, and engaged. It becomes a process that permits the individual to ask the questions of not just who am I but also what am I in relation to others and to the world in which I have journeyed all these numerous years. The aging process by its very nature fosters a deepening personal spiritual development by drawing a person through the spiritual tasks of discovering, pondering, integrating, surrendering, growing, and companioning.

The years of life have the power to become a transcendent time for deeper prayer that moves beyond the confines of the self to a place where mystery and discovery coexist. To this end, the aging process could be likened to a journey. The start of any journey encompasses both the anticipation and the hope of reaching one's final destination. The journey begins out of a desire to connect in a particular way with someone or something at a given location and culminates upon reaching that destination. As a result of this desire the pilgrimage often becomes more than its destination because it becomes the very pathway upon which one travels. This process occurs because the pilgrim often undergoes the process of transformation as part of the journey. No matter what the purpose of the pilgrimage, one must have some idea of what one is searching for, even if the vagueness of the reason often overshadows the clarity of the purpose. Like the pilgrimage begun out of the desire to connect, the natural process of aging extends to each person the invitation to connect with one's true self, which Christian spirituality claims can only be understood in relationship to God.

Discovering

The process of aging, first of all, is a discovery process. At some point, we discover that we are aging. We may have less energy to do the things we used to routinely do because the tasks we used to perform so easily now require some mindful attention. It is through this discovery process that we realize the fact that just as things have changed so have we changed. Perhaps the roles we occupied in life are diminished and in some cases no longer relevant. Perhaps it is the areas of our lives that we paid little attention to that now come to the forefront of our consciousness. We may begin to question what all the passing years have meant and begin to search for answers to all that is changing both within us and around us. We discover that the previous ways of doing no longer work for us. We must develop new strategies, make new adjustments to how we have functioned in the past, and adapt ourselves to these events and situations.

This discovery process affects all aspects of our being. At some point in our lives, most often in moments of crisis, we are thrown into a crisis of faith where all that we have previously known no longer provides us with the assurance it once did. Sociologists refer to these moments as states of anomie or "norm-lessness." The known ways of responding and functioning give way to the unknown. It is through such moments that many of us come into contact with that deeper side of ourselves. Such moments call for a transcendent response involving a deep reaffirmation of the value of worth of each one of us (Seeber, 1999). At such times, we may ask ourselves what this all means or who I am as a result of this situation or event. In such moments we discover what it is that moves us, what has and does give our lives purpose. The gifts we have been given over the course of our lifetime take on a new focus for us that may lead to what Eric Erikson termed generativity, the desire to share those gifts with those that come after us. It is through the process of discovery one encounters the deepest side of the self. An inner place that searches, calls out, and longs to be heard. Perhaps it is the desire to be assured that we are not alone on the journey of life, as well as the discovery of what that unique journey has meant not only to us but also to those with whom we have come in contact along the way.

The point of discovery in one's spiritual development originates from the place that rests deep at the core of one's being. It is a place whose unfamiliarity causes one to pause in guarded reluctance before embarking upon its path. Often the arrival at such a place is met with reluctance and distress, in part because we have been acculturated to believe that we must have the answers to all the questions life presents to us as opposed to allowing ourselves, in the words of the poet Rilke, to "*live* the questions." In that pausing, the existence of paradox is realized. It is the paradox that in the unknown areas of the self is where we are our most authentic, most real and most alive. For in that place, the essence of the true self is revealed which, more times than not, has been camouflaged, hidden, and masked as a result of the experiences, interactions, and events of a lifetime.

This formative task of discovery has been a central element to a number of spiritualities over the centuries. Its centrality is in part due to the innate human need to know what will befall one. To dwell in mystery is difficult. Our human nature is one that likes order, structure, and planning. We long to know the answers to our questions, many times even before the questions are asked. This discovery, this realization that change has occurred both within us and around us is an element that both aging and spirituality share. The journey of discovery is never a one-time endeavor but rather it becomes a way of life. In order for one to embark one must prepare for the endeavor through practice. The wisdom of the early Christian church proposed that such a practice involves the discipline of "paying attention," thereby enabling the individual to overcome the blockages in life that serve as a hindrance to receiving grace. Attention, according to this tradition, was to be focused on three areas: the self–the place where one was to embrace the beauty of one's own soul; death–recalling that the only gift one is given is the present moment; and God–the source of all life. By developing this practice the individual is transformed into the image and likeness of God. The very act of fully embracing life or living mindfully enables this transformation to occur because one is able to catch glimpses of one's divinity as the moments of life unfold. The end result of this transformative process, according to the spirituality of the early church, is "freedom from care."

Pondering

In her book, *Kitchen Table Wisdom*, Rachel Naomi Remen, MD (1996) writes that "we carry with us every story we have ever heard and every story we have ever lived, filed away at some deep place in our memory." Some of these stories are good and others are not, but they all provide us with insight into the mystery of who we are and what we are called to become. The process of aging is itself a story. For some, it may be a long drawn out one with numerous twists and turns while for others it may be relatively short and seemingly uneventful. But as Remen notes, in knowing our individual stories we are required to have an inner experience of as well as a personal response to life (Remen, 1996).

At some point in our lives we come to a place within ourselves that allows us the freedom to listen to the stories of our lives and ponder the lessons they have to teach us. In their book *A Passion for Life*, Anne Brennan and Janice Brewi (2000) state that "age gives us a perspective to re-evaluate, re-interpret, re-found, re-claim, re-member our own story." To ponder one's own story validates one's lived experiences by affording the opportunity to relive anew the ups and downs, the joys and sorrows as well as the achievements and failures. As a result of this reliving, one comes to a place of deeper understanding as to what all the seemingly unrelated events of life have meant.

In order to ponder our own unique stories, we must allow ourselves the freedom to become present to them. We need to focus ourselves and draw our attention inward as we reexamine the events of our lives. One of the first steps in this process is the need to quiet ourselves from the all too distracting noises that surround us, the outer ones as well as the inner ones. In the words of Paul Tournier, "modern people lack silence. They no longer lead their own lives; they are dragged along by events. . . . Silence has the power to force you to dig deep inside yourself " (Foster, 2000). We find ourselves in the act of "digging deeply" when we are able to still our thoughts and slowly, slowly, begin to discover that this silent time makes us quiet and deepens our awareness of ourselves and God (Nouwen, 1975). As a result we enable ourselves to engage in the second step, the act of reminiscence.

To reminisce is to recall a past experience or episode of our life. Robert Butler in 1963 stated that reminiscence was a central component in what he termed the process of life-review. This process occurs as the events of one's life are reviewed, surveyed, observed, and reflected upon. Butler notes:

> Reconsideration of previous experiences and their meanings occurs, often with the concomitant revised or expanded understanding. Such reorganization of past experiences may provide a more valid picture, giving new and significant meanings to one's life. It may also prepare one for death. (Butler, 1963)

In the act of our re-calling these moments and events we soon recognize that they hold before us the possibilities for greater self-knowledge and deeper understanding which serve to mark the third step, the process of making meaning.

Victor Frankl, author of *Man's Search for Meaning*, termed the process of meaning making *Logotherapy*. Frankl contends that human beings are unique, spiritual, and by nature, responsible. For Frankl, meaning is discovered in the events of our lives in three ways: (a) as a result of those areas of our lives which we have shared with others; (b) the ways in which we have been shaped and formed by the world around us in terms of our values and beliefs; and (c) in our attitudes to the situations of life in which we have no control (Frankl, 1986).

By engaging in the formative task of pondering life's experiences, we come to a greater appreciation of them. We come to see the interconnectedness of the often-segregated pieces of our lives and the ways in which they have brought us to this place in time. Our stories serve as guideposts along our journey, mapping out for us the terrain we've covered with all its valleys, flatlands, and deserts. We learn that our memories tell us we came from somewhere, we have traveled through time and now take our place in the present, and it is in the present we must live (White Eagle, 1999).

Integrating

Our pondering of life's events leads us to greater clarity and calls us to a deeper understanding of these events and their impact upon us. We begin to integrate the various aspects of our lives and through this process of integration come to see the interconnectedness of all our life experiences. The great twentieth-century Catholic theologin Karl Rahner touched on this issue of integration in his response to a question asked him regarding how he found old age. Rahner summed it up in the following manner:

> A peaceful, ripe old age, an old age with wisdom, a beautiful old age perhaps in which one reminisces, does exist. But, quite soberly, the sort of old age that steadily draws near to death exists too–an old age in which one is exhausted. (Rahner, 1985)

Rahner, in a somewhat stark and stoic Germanic manner, addresses one of the key issues regarding spirituality the later years bring, namely the need for integration. The situation faced by older adults in contemporary society can easily appear to be a two-edged sword. On one account society clearly states that anything to do with the aging process, particularly those areas that speak of decline or impending death, are to be avoided at all cost. In the same vein, individuals are being challenged to accept life's last decades as a period of time for leisure and enjoyment of a life well lived. It becomes a time to be embraced with gusto that fills the individual with rich possibilities for new adventure, deeper insight and sustained life. This dualistic view is, in part, because we've tended to view the life course in linear terms as moving from birth to death. The longer the line between the two, the more successful the individual becomes. Our whole contemporary Western Culture is based on this model to the extent that much of the notion of successful aging revolves around activities and achievements. Our medical practices, for example, are all aimed at eliminating disease, thereby lengthening the life span.

This view of human development, however, is not universal by any means. In other cultures, a different view of human development exists in which life is seen in circular terms. Each phase begins and completes itself before the next phase of life begins. The end of one phase merely means the beginning of another. In this view, success is measured by the manner in which the individual has gained an understanding of the self at each phase of development, one's unique place in society and the role one was to ultimately occupy. It was the way in which the individual embraced each phase of life that determined success, because the direct result of fully embracing each phase of life translated into the achievement of deeper self-knowledge.

When we are young our desire to experience all that life has to offer often compels us to seek adventure, to make our mark, fulfill our wildest hopes and dreams. Life presents itself as ours to explore, conquer and claim. Swiftly we glide through the years, experiencing the ups and downs while eagerly awaiting the new adventures yet to unfold. Often, we do not take the time to fully embrace a moment before moving on to another. There's simply too much to accomplish, too much to explore, too much to do. Inevitably, as Mary Hester Valentine, SSND, notes, "our age, however, can be ignored and protected against for only so long; sooner or later we are caught up in the web of years, and are forced to be as old as we are" (Valentine, 1994). The moment emerges when the rapid pace in which we've journeyed begins to slow. In that slowing pace, our vision changes, as the desire to live in the future doesn't present itself with as much urgency as before. Our hearing changes, as the din of accomplishment, ambition, and status gives way to the quiet whispers of our past inviting us to listen and learn. Our journey gradually becomes a quest for deeper integration. It is an integration that weaves together the often mismatched events of our lives, creating a pattern and design that is uniquely our own. It becomes our own masterpiece ripe with meaning, purpose, and fulfillment. It is this journey, then, towards deeper integration that becomes one of the central issues faced by older adults. It is a journey whose mystery unfolds more deeply with each passing year.

The journey may contain highlights of a life lived fully or disappointments that we have experienced over the years. Perhaps they are the memories of events long forgotten which the years have tucked neatly away for us. Whatever these moments and events may be, they contain the ability to be our most powerful guides into the last quarter of life. The formative impact they have had on us and our response to them has brought us to the place we are at this moment in our lives. In the words of Mary Hester Valentine, SSND, "we are old because God wills us to be, and although we cannot see the reason, there is one . . . and as Cardinal Newman said, '[God] knows what [God] is about' (Valentine, 1994). It is in both the recalling and the naming of them that they become held in an honored place and proclaimed sacred. For they have been our companions, our teachers, and our mentors. It is with the passing of years that we come to the realization of the importance of gathering all that we have done and seen; all that we have experienced and how that has shaped us into who and what we have become; of who and what we are. In so doing, we become witnesses to God's presence at work in our lives and in the sum of all we are.

Surrendering

Another formative task that is integrally connected to the aging process is that of surrendering. As Kathleen Fisher notes in her book, *Winter Grace*:

> Aging is both descent and ascent, both loss and gain. At every point in the human journey we find that we have to let go in order to move forward; and letting go means dying a little. (Fisher, 1985)

We physically let go of possessions, of ways of doing things, of people who have provided us with both support and comfort. We term this letting go "loss." Our perception is that as a direct result of losing such things we are in return lessened. The very act of aging involves the relinquishment of possessions, people, and places. It can be a fearful time in our lives. This process of letting go accompanies the changes that we have discovered occurring within our bodies and in the world around us. Perhaps this manifests itself in the act of relinquishing familiar routines, cherished possessions, and valued individuals. All too often the focus is placed upon that which is relinquished rather than what may now be available to us in its place.

We are acculturated into a belief system that stresses the importance of acquisition. To not have is to lessen our value as productive human beings. The more we have, the greater we become. Not having is equated with weakness and vulnerability. We come to appropriate the various aspects of our lives, whether they be people or things. In this appropriation we overlook the reality that these things were given to us as gifts.

The whole of our lives have been filled with gifts that were freely given and received. We have convinced ourselves that our inmost value rests in the possessions we have acquired and we deserve these things purely because they are there. Jane Thibault, in her book, *A Deepening*

Love Affair: The Gift of God in Later Life, refers to the reluctance of letting go as stemming from "a fear that God will not provide us with enough of what we need. And, as a result, it is a settling for less than we are called to be given" (Thibault, 1983, p. 47).

The prayer of Ignatius of Loyola touches upon this theme of God's benevolence and our response in the face of loss. In his *Spiritual Exercises*, Ignatius encourages us to contemplate the blessings God has so freely bestowed upon us throughout the course of our lives. As a result of that contemplation we would be given both the insight and grace to say:

> Take, O Lord, all my liberty. Receive in their entirety my memory, intellect and will. And since whatever else I have or hold you have given to me so I give everything back to you to be managed entirely according to your preference. To me give only your love and your grace, and with these I am rich enough and want nothing more. (Delmage, 1968)

In the midst of surrender and loss, we turn in trust toward God with hope and assurance that life will not end but will continue to flourish and move us into a new place in our lives and in the world around us.

An important aspect of our surrendering process includes the act of forgiveness. There are situations and events in our lives where we made mistakes and faltered on life's journey. In our admission of these mistakes and shortcomings we come to a greater understanding of our own humanness. There are relationships in our lives that have been damaged or in some cases completely severed. The issues that led to the conflict with another may not have been resolved and the brokenness of the relationship still hangs over us and weighs us down. Often we withhold our forgiveness to protect ourselves or even to impose our sense of justice on the other. What we often fail to realize is that in so doing we often place restrictions upon our own growth and development. The act of forgiveness also entails the realization that we, too, played a part in the conflict. We will find it difficult to forgive our offender as long as we do not take ownership of our own contributions to the misunderstandings and conflicts (Schachter-Shalomi, 1995). Forgiveness also entails forgiving ourselves for the choices we made as well as the options we relinquished and never acted upon. Circumstances at given points of our lives led to the decisions we made. Perhaps we had limited information and had to decide what was best for us at that given moment in time. Sometimes, in hindsight, we come to regret the decision we made, and the questions of "what if" and "why did I" weigh heavily upon us. In our self-forgiveness we often come to realize that we did what we could with the information and the circumstances life presented to us. The need exists for us to embrace these painful moments of life with compassion and allow ourselves to see them in a new light as having served as guideposts along our journey. For out of all the decisions we made there exists the opportunity for both grace and growth that serve to move us further along the journey of life.

I recall a phone call I received a few years ago from Alice, an 86-year-old resident of one of the retirement communities where I once worked. Alice has, over the years, become part of my family and she called to tell me that she had put herself on the waiting list to move into the assisted living unit. She stated she did so because her physical energy was decreasing more and more and she found it difficult to do almost everything. I went to see her the day following her move. She said she had spent the greater part of the day adjusting to her new surroundings. They were smaller than her previous accommodations. She stated that she had spent the morning going through old letters and cards and discarding them. "It's funny," she said, "I always kept these things and now I'm giving them up and even though I've cried my way through this morning . . . it feels freeing to simplify things. I just wonder . . . did I do it right? Life I mean . . . did I do it right? That concerns me."

Alice's reflections on the events of her life and the concern she expressed as to whether or not she had "done it right" is part of our human condition. Throughout the centuries individuals have mulled over the events of their lives in their attempts to find both meaning and purpose. Both the aging process and spirituality appear to draw this task of life review to the surface. One recalls, remembers, and attempts to put the intricate pieces of life's jigsaw puzzle together. In the processing of these memories and events one begins to make sense out of the previously daunting mystery life had perhaps been. One is able to see more clearly the working of grace as the darkest moments of life are illuminated in a new way. One is able to empathize with the musings of Florida Scott Maxwell,

> You need only claim the events of your life to make yourself yours. When you truly possess all you have been and done, which may take some time, you are fierce with reality. When at last age has assembled you together, will it not be easy to let it all go, lived, balanced, over? (Scott-Maxwell, 1968)

Growing

The book *Tuesdays with Morrie* chronicles the last months of life of Morrie Schwartz and the re-established relationship with one of his former students, Mich Albom. In the book, Morrie shares his thoughts about life's meaning and purpose, the importance of relationships, and the need for continual growth. One day, Mich asks the following:

> Aging is not just decay, you know. It's growth. It's more than the negative that you're going to die; it's also that positive that you understand that you're going to die, and that you live a better life because of it. (Albom, 1997)

Morrie's statements regarding growth illustrate the fact that one holds the potential to grow and develop no matter what the circumstances of life or how old a person may be. This invitation to continued growth calls one to recognize that life does not end because one has accumulated years, but rather, life continues to be lived, explored and claimed. Through this process one comes to the realization that one's past experiences give birth to new opportunities. They are the opportunities to experience teaching moments that call us to explore new territories, embrace the unknown, and challenge us to stretch beyond our own perceived limitations, but only if we choose to do so. Psychologist Carl Jung terms this process of growth *individuation* and defines it as

> a spontaneous, natural process within the psyche; it is potentially present in every person, although most are unaware of it. Unless it is inhibited, obstructed, or distorted by some specific disturbance, it is a process of maturation or unfolding, the psychic parallel to the physical process of growth and aging. (Jung, 1933)

It is a process through which an individual comes to a greater awareness of the self by gradually shedding the masks that have been used throughout life to reveal to others only a tiny fragment of the true self. The process of growth calls a person to embrace the uniqueness of one's life as well as the situations and the events that have occurred to form the person into a unique being. Growth then calls the person to celebrate that uniqueness, for no other individual has experienced the exact same set of circumstances, was influenced by the same things or encountered similar mentors throughout life. Growth becomes both a journey and a pilgrimage through the hallowed ground of one's own life, taking one back to the core of one's own being. Growth then is not entirely a solitary process but rather one that occurs within the context of community. An individual grows back to the core of the self not just for one's own benefit but also for the benefit of others. As Carl Jung states:

> A human being would certainly not grow to be seventy- or eighty-years-old if this longevity had no meaning for the species to which he belongs. The afternoon of human life must also have a significance of its own and cannot be merely a pitiful appendage to life's morning. (Jung, 1933)

Deep within a seed, just as deep within each individual, rests all that is needed for growth. The potential lies hidden away patiently waiting for the right set of circumstances to converge in order for the growth to occur. A real life example of this is Elizabeth, who at age 85 and struggling to find something to occupy the long days left void by her retirement from teaching stumbles upon an advertisement for a local massage school. She enrolls in the classes and becomes a massage therapist providing the gift of healing touch to her fellow community members in the retirement center as well as former students and colleagues. At times, we may be surprised by what grows out of our lives as we survey the new endeavors we have successfully embarked upon, the new skills we have developed, and the new knowledge we have gained. The later years of life then contain the invitation to move forward into an unknown place that grows slowly within us, bearing its roots and breaking forth through the rich fertile soil that is life.

Companioning

The final formative task we will explore involves the self in relation to others. For the process of spiritual development is as much a personal one as it is communal. We are integrally connected to all that is around us. The spiritual tasks serve to take an individual deeper into the depths. of the authentic self, stripped of the masks and falsehoods that have existed over a lifetime, in order to come in contact with the real. In so doing, we come to a greater understanding of what our lives have meant, not only to us but also to those around us. The task of going deeper into the self is not done in order for the individual to remain there, but rather it is done so the individual may share the knowledge of what he/she has learned with the larger community.

An elder tale from the Athabascan nation of Alaska illustrates this notion of companioning as it unfolds in the lives of two old women (Wallis, 1993). The tribe had supported both women for years. Everything they wanted, even when these wants were to the detriment of others in the tribe, were given to them out of deep respect for their advanced age. One year a terrible famine occurs and the tribe is forced to make the decision to leave their territory in search of food. The chief informs the old women that the tribe can no longer support them and they are to be left behind to die. As they are left behind, each one goes through a period of deep inner searching as she prepares for her approaching death. As a result of this inner work, each comes to new insights into the gift of life and its meaning. A lifetime of experiences and skill, long abandoned by each woman's internalized helplessness, comes to the forefront. As a result each woman makes a conscious decision to live and uses the knowledge she has gained throughout life to ensure her own survival. As a team, they survive the period of famine as well as the harshness of the seasons and grow in deeper appreciation of their uniqueness and wisdom. By reaching into the depths of their own uniqueness, each woman contributed to her own as well as the other's survival and transformation. Each was taken back to the core of her own being and in so doing discovered the seed of her own potential and ability.

This process of gathering and distributing the wealth of a life lived amidst struggle, triumph, joy, and sorrow is a communal process. By engaging in it one realizes that our individual stories become the communal story, with each one serving as a tiny piece of the entire whole. We soon realize that we are connected with all that has been and all that will be and our lived experiences illustrate that fact. We recognize that, like the stories of those who have gone before us, the events, situations, and interactions of our lives have become our legacy and a testimonial to our very being.

RECOMMENDED READINGS

Address, R. F., & Person, H. E. (2003). *That you may live long: Caring for our aging parents, caring for ourselves.* New York: URJ Press.

Alborn, M. (1997). *Tuesdays with Morrie.* New York: Doubleday. p. 118.

Brennan, A., & Brewi, J. (2000). *Passion for life.* New York: Continuum. p. 116.

Butler, R. (1963). *Life review: An interpretation of reminiscence in the aged.* 1963 Psychiatry, Vol. 26: 655-676.

Delmage, L. (1968). *The spiritual exercises of St. Ignatius Loyola: An American translation.* NJ: Joseph F. Wagner, Inc., page 122.

Eckhart, M. (1983). *Meditations with Meister Eckhart* (M. Fox, Trans.). Santa Fe: Bear and Company.

Erikson, E. (1998). *The life cycle completed.* New York: Norton Paperback.

Fischer, K. (1998). *Winter grace.* Nashville: Upper Room Press, p. 4.

Foster, R., & Griffin, E. (2000). *Spiritual classics.* San Francisco: Harper Books, p. 160.

Fowler, J. (1995). *Stages of faith: The psychology of human development.* San Francisco: Harper and Row.

Frankl, V. (1959). *Man's search for meaning.* New York: Simon and Shuster.

Frankl, V. (1986). *The doctor and the soul: From psychotherapy to logotherapy.* New York: Vintage Books.

Guenther, M. (1992). *Holy listening: The art of spiritual direction.* Cambridge: Cowley Publications.

Huber, L. (2003). *Revelations on the road: A pilgrim journey.* Boulder: Word Woven Press.

Jung, C. G. (1933). *Modern man in search of a soul.* New York: Harcourt-Brace.

Kurtz, E., & Ketcham, K. (1992). *The spirituality of imperfection.* New York: Bantam Trade Paperback. 293 total.

Merton, T. (1993). *Thoughts in solitude.* Boston: Shambhala Pocket Classics, p. 37.

Miller, J. (1995). *Autumn wisdom: Finding meaning in life's later years.* Minneapolis: Augsburg Press.

Moody, H., & Carroll, D. (1997). *The five stages of the soul.* New York: Anchor Books.

Nouwen, H. (1975). *Reaching out: Solitude and silence.* New York: Doubleday and Company.

Palmer, P. J. (2000). *Let your life speak: Listening to the voice of vocation.* New York: Jossey-Bass Publishers, p. 3.

Rahner, K. (1985). *I remember.* New York: Crossroads. p. 102.

Remen, R. N. (1996). *Kitchen table wisdom.* New York: Riverhead Books, p. xxix.

Remen, R. N. (2000). *My grandfather's blessing–Stories of strength, refuge, and belonging.* New York: Riverhead Books.

Rilke, R. M. (1934). *Letters to a young poet,* translation by M.D. Herter Norton.

Schachter-Shalomi, Z. (1995). *From age-ing to sage-ing.* New York: Warner Books.

Scott-Maxwell, F. (1968). *The measure of my days.* New York: Penguin Books, p. 42.

Seeber, J. (1999). A Deep and Chronic Spiritual Crisis. In J. W. Ellor, S. McFadden, & S. Sapp (Eds.), *Aging and spirituality: The first decade.* San Francisco: American Society on Aging.

Smith, H. (2001). *Why religion matters: The fate of the human spirit in an age of disbelief.* San Francisco: Harper and Row.

Standish, N. G., & McCormack, E. (2001). Formative Spirituality. *Presence: The Journal of Spiritual Directors International, 17*(1).

Thibault, J. M. (1993). *A deepening love affair, the gift of God in later life.* Nashville: Upper Room Press.

Valentine, M. H. (1994). *Aging in the Lord.* New York: Paulist Press, p. 1 & p. 18.

Wallis, V. (1993). *Two old women: An Alaska legend of betrayal, courage, and survival.* New York: Harper Perennial.

Watkins, D. (2004). *Practical theology for aging.* Binghamton: The Haworth Press, Inc.

White Eagle, P. (1999). Storytelling. In J. W. Ellor, S. McFadden, & S. Sapp (Eds.), *Aging and spirituality: The first decade.* San Francisco: American Society on Aging.

York, S. (2001). *Pilgrim heart: The inner journey home.* San Francisco: Jossey-Bass Inc.

Spiritual Need Two:
Continued Learning for Older Adults and Older Adult Organizations

Rod Parrott, MDiv, MA

SUMMARY. Age provides opportunity not only for a person to grow spiritually, but also for people to enlarge their understandings of the world about them, including God, and connect them to previous learnings and life-experiences. In older age, learning is not merely an affirmation of what has been, but a re-creation of the self in relation to everything that surrounds the person. The theories of James Fowler, Malcom Knowles, Peter Senge, and Erik Erikson provide insight as to the purpose of older adult education. The goal is for churchs to encourage and assist in each person's re-construction of their lives as they view life from the perspective of length of years. Concrete examples of re-constructive learning are provided. *[Article copies available for a fee from The Haworth Document Delivery Service: 1-800-HAWORTH. E-mail address: <docdelivery@haworthpress.com> Website: <http://www.HaworthPress.com> © 2005 by The Haworth Press, Inc. All rights reserved.]*

KEYWORDS. Spirituality, learning, learning theories, conjunctive, universalizing, new ways of learning, re-constructive

---

[Haworth co-indexing entry note]: "Spiritual Need Two: Continued Learning for Older Adults and Older Adult Organizations." Parrott, Rod. Co-published simultaneously in *Journal of Religion, Spirituality & Aging* (The Haworth Pastoral Press, an imprint of The Haworth Press, Inc.) Vol. 17, No. 3/4, 2005, pp. 73-85; and: *Ministering to Older Adults: The Building Blocks* (ed: Donald R. Koepke) The Haworth Pastoral Press, an imprint of The Haworth Press, Inc., 2005, pp. 73-85. Single or multiple copies of this article are available for a fee from The Haworth Document Delivery Service [1-800-HAWORTH, 9:00 a.m. - 5:00 p.m. (EST). E-mail address: docdelivery@haworthpress.com].

Available online at http://www.haworthpress.com/web/JRSA
2005 by The Haworth Press, Inc. All rights reserved.
doi:10.1300/J496v17n03_07

Since the epidemic of psychosocial and educational studies of the human life cycle that peaked in the 1970s,[1] it has been commonly accepted that older adulthood is a time in which persons are particularly free to continue learning. Although most studies, aware of wide situational diversity, are careful not to identify a particular chronological age with the onset of such activity, it is nonetheless suggested that by mid-life, when persons have established themselves with respect to vocation, family, residence, and other elements commonly understood to be part of the human agenda, when, as it were, their "plates" are cleared of some of the necessities of life they are open to movement into non-material matters: to spirituality, to service, to altruism, and philanthropy, to a sustained quest for meaning. Although such an assumption indulges a well-worn tension between the material and the spiritual, and certainly needs to be more carefully studied, it remains true that older adulthood may provide a time when the inner need to establish one's place socially or economically has abated. The pressure is off, and attention and energy can be given to other pursuits, including the fuller development of the self.

This common opportunity presented by age, along with a general increase in attention to spirituality, has given rise to persons within some religious communities to investigate the spiritual development of older adults. In the present chapter the author proposes to connect the literature in human development to that in religious education, believing that while there actually is an overlap in the two areas, spirituality and education, they remain, for many church members, somewhat disconnected.

Within the historic religious vocations of the Catholic church there is a long and distinguished history of spiritual formation and/or spiritual direction, while among Protestant congregations there has been a different kind of adult education since at least the Sunday School movement of the late 19th and early 20th centuries. The current interest in spirituality is occurring largely outside the traditional educational structures of Protestant churches, just as it also is occurring among the laity of the Catholic church. In either case, the time is ripe for a consideration of the nature of older adult education in the church.

While certainly not unreceptive to a focused study of the spiritual disciplines, as they are generally called, our subject in this chapter is a much broader range of activity that could simply be called "education" or learning. It is not our intention to exclude education in spiritual disciplines, but neither are those disciplines our primary focus.

This may appear to be a disappointing choice, since on the surface the basic metaphors of spirituality and education seem quite different: spirituality, after all, has to do with the air and breath and respiration, taking in what is necessary for life; education is associated with child-rearing as a forming or in-forming *(duc're)*, or, some say, with a leading forth *(dü're)* (Oxford Dictionary, 1971, I. 833, II. 2967-2968). But such appearances mask a more fundamental similarity. Spirituality and education really are partners; two means, some would say one is natural, the other, man-made, by which human beings relate to the larger world around them, including God, and develop and realize themselves in that relationship. Hence one could argue from one to the other in either direction: spirituality is a form of education; education is a form of spirituality. No matter how one approaches it, education and spirituality belong together.

THEORIES OF ADULT DEVELOPMENT

This is not the place for a discussion of the contemporary theories of education, particularly of the varieties of ways in which people learn. Most of us know that there are linear learners and gestalt learners, visual learners and auditory learners, etc. We know of savants whose learning in music or mathematics outstrips their learning in other areas, including social skills (as, for example, in the movies *Rain Man* and *A Beautiful Mind*). Most recently, we have added emotional learning. Given these diverse ways of learning as a caveat, there is a general consensus that adults continue to gather and process information and experience through the entire life cycle, i.e., they learn all life long.

Such learning, of course, is not an automatic accompaniment of aging. Among the various studies of psychological, cognitive, moral, or faith development stages, we know of none that suggests that it is so. Certain social pressures may block or ease such learning, but in every situation, the person must choose to learn. In all learning theories there are some correlations between various stages or levels, but those correlations for the most part underline the need for completing the tasks of one level or stage before moving on to a subsequent one. Admittedly there are some "thresholds," both chronological and social, at which certain tasks become do-able, but most of the understandings of how people learn do not attach them to specific ages.

Having said all this, we cite the fifth and sixth stages of faith development in James Fowler's *Stages of Faith* as a central reference point. Fowler locates these stages, which he calls "conjunctive" and "universalizing" faith, respectively, in mid-life or later adulthood. Here are his two somewhat extensive descriptions of them:

> Stage 5 Conjunctive faith involves the integration into self and outlook of much that was suppressed or unrecognized in the interest of Stage 4's self-certainty and conscious cognitive and affective adaptation to reality. This stage develops a "second naiveté" (Ricoeur) in which symbolic power is reunited with conceptual meanings. Here there must also be a new reclaiming and reworking of one's past. There must be an opening to the voices of one's "deeper self." Importantly, this involves a critical recognition of one's social unconscious–the myths, ideal images and prejudices built deeply into the self-system by virtue of one's nurture within a particular social class, religious tradition, ethnic group or the like.

Unusual before mid-life, Stage 5 knows the sacrament of defeat and the reality of irrevocable commitments and acts. What the previous stage struggled to clarify, in terms of the boundaries of the self and outlook, this stage now makes porous and permeable. Alive to paradox and the truth in apparent contradictions, this stage strives to unify opposites in mind and experience. It generates and maintains vulnerability to the strange truths of those who are "other." Ready for closeness to that which is different and threatening to self and outlook (including new depths of experience in spirituality and religious revelation), this stage's commitment to justice is freed from the confines of tribe, class, religious community, or nation. And with the seriousness that can arise when life is more than half over, this stage is ready to spend and be spent for the cause of conserving and cultivating the possibility of others' generating identity and meaning.

The new strength of this stage comes in the rise of the ironic imagination–a capacity to see and be in one's or one's group's most powerful meanings, while simultaneously recognizing that they are relative, partial and inevitably distorting apprehensions of transcendent reality. Its danger lies in the direction of a paralyzing passivity or inaction, giving rise to complacency or cynical withdrawal, due to its paradoxical understanding of truth.

Stage 5 can appreciate symbols, myths and rituals (its own and others') because it has been grasped, in some measure, by the depth of reality to which they refer. It also sees the divisions of the human family vividly because it has been apprehended by the possibility (and imperative) of an inclusive community of being. But this stage remains divided. It lives and acts between an untransformed world and a transforming vision and loyalties. In some few cases this division yields to the call of the radical actualization that we call Stage 6 (Fowler, *Stages*, 1995, 197-198).

Stage 6 is exceedingly rare. The persons best described by it have generated faith compositions in which their felt sense of an ultimate environment is inclusive of all being. They have become incarnators and actualizers of the spirit of an inclusive and fulfilled human community.

They are "contagious" in the sense that they create zones of liberation from the social, political, economic, and ideological shackles we place and endure on human futurity. Living with felt participation in a power that unifies and transforms the world, Universalizers are often experienced as subversive of the structures (including religious structures) by which we sustain our individual and corporate survival, security, and significance. Many persons in this stage die at the hands of those whom they hope to change. Universalizers are often persons who may be described by this stage to have a special grace that makes them seem more lucid, more simple, and yet somehow more fully human than the rest of us. Their community is universal in extent. Particularities are cherished because they are vessels of the universal, and thereby valuable apart from any utilitarian considerations. Life is both loved and held to loosely. Such persons are ready for fellowship with persons at any of the other stages and from any other faith tradition (Fowler, 1979, 200-201).

Now as we noted earlier, Fowler locates Stage 5 in mid-life and onward; Stage 6, he assigns to older adults. In common parlance, we would translate "conjunctive" and "universalizing" faith as, respectively, "putting it all together," "making some sense of the whole," and "living self-lessly [or generously?] in the world."

With such definitions, we should note that while both conjunctive and universalizing faith are possible for older adults from mid-life onward, Fowler describes Stage 6 as "very rare." Although he resists the language, Fowler in one place hints that people in Stage 6 are "saints," (Fowler, 1995, 202) and Thomas Groome, in his summation of Fowler, explicitly uses the term. As examples of Stage 6 people, Fowler lists Mother Teresa, Gandhi, Martin Luther King, Jr., Dag Hammarskjold, Dietrich Bonhoeffer, Abraham Herschel, and Thomas Merton.

It is intriguing that some of these examples of the latter are relatively young. Mother Teresa arrived at a sense of her self-giving vocation as a nun at the age 33. Dietrich Bonhoeffer was executed at age 39. Martin Luther King, Jr., was assassinated at age 39. These were not "older adults," but relatively young middle-agers.

The clue, of course, is that everyone's "state of union with God" has a slightly different shape. What is common to them all is a kind of self-m emptying that is expressed in the early Christian hymn Paul cites in Philippians 2:5-11, where instead of "grasping" or clinging to his "God-ness" for "dear life," Jesus empties himself, taking on the form of a servant (slave), becoming obedient even to death on a cross. When one considers that core character trait or activity, two things are clear: (1) one ought not be intimidated by Fowler's short Stage 6 list, and (2) it would be a shame to limit sainthood to such public figures. There are, in every community, ordinary, older, non-famous adults who have put aside their own personal interests and live constantly for others.

Characteristics of Adult Teaching/Learning

In his chapter in a recent book on continuing education in the church (Roberts, 2000, 67-79), D. Bruce Roberts employs the story of the apostle Paul in Athens (Acts, 17) to outline four components of an adult teaching/learning situation: (1) identifying a problem or issue to address; (2) engaging persons in conversation that raises questions and challenges perspectives; (3) structuring more formal ways to engage the questions and issues; and (4) engaging persons from the perspective of their own experience (Roberts, 2000, 67).

As Roberts goes on to show, a similar list of aspects can be found in Malcolm Knowles' work on adult education (Malcolm Knowles, 1980). Knowles lists four "assumptions" about adult learners: (1) they understand themselves to be independent and self-directing; (2) they bring experience and knowledge to learning activities; (3) they are interested in questions or problems which relate to their own lives; and (4) they focus on here-and-now tasks and problems (Roberts, 2000, 69-70). Roberts offers two "hunches" about adult learning that are worth remembering: (1) an important factor in adult learning is the matter of *control*: adults want to be in control of their learning; and (2) adult learners are interested in *ways of learning* that can be used with different issues or problems (Roberts, 2000, 71-72). Following Stephen Brook- field, he calls this "critical thinking" (Roberts, 2000, 72).

This view of adult learning applies differently across the many life situations of the older adult, whether one uses the language of "young old," "old," and "very old," or "active," "transitional," and "frail." The challenge to the religious educator is to define learning activities suited to specific situations, yet which reflect core understandings of the person as continuing learner.

Helping the Church Learn About Older Adult Learning

That older adults have different learning needs has implications not only for individual older adults themselves, but for the organization and development of older adult ministries: as older adults need to continue learning, so do the organizations that work with them. Once we abandon the stereotypical model of aging as a loss of powers, we can begin to re-shape the church's educational structures that work with older adults.

A helpful tool in this re-shaping is Peter Senge's work on "learning organizations." This is not the place for a detailed discussion of Senge's proposals–"the five disciplines," "organizational learning disabilities," or "the laws of the fifth discipline." Senge has written more than enough about them in the 400 pages of his initial book (Senge, 1990) and a subsequent 600-page "fieldbook" (Senge, 1994). Suffice it to say that he proposes building continuing learning into the "system" of whatever organization is in view. (His purview is primarily business, but the principles can be applied in other settings as well.) The following excerpts are illustrative of his interest:

> At the heart of the learning organization is a shift of mind–from seeing ourselves as separate from the world to connected to the world, from seeing problems as caused by someone or something "out there" to seeing how our own actions create the problems we experience. A learning organization is a place where people are continually discovering how they create their reality. And how they can change it. (Senge, 1994, Discipline 12-13)

> Real learning gets to the heart of what it means to be human. Through learning we re-create ourselves. Through learning we become able to do something we never were able to do. Through learning we extend our capacity to create, to be part of the generative process of life. There is within each of us a deep hunger for this type of learning. (Senge, 1994, 14)

> This, then, is the basic meaning of a "learning organization"–an organization that is continually expanding its capacity to create its future. For such an organization, it is not enough merely to survive. "Survival learning" or what is more often termed "adaptive learning" is important–indeed it is necessary. But for a learning organization, "adaptive learning" must be joined by "generative

learning," learning that enhances our capacity to create. (Senge, 1994, 14)

For a book aimed at business, or perhaps also non-profits, this language coheres amazingly well with the kinds of ideals and values articulated in religious education circles. (Early in his book Senge actually references the Christian use of the term *metanoia* ["repent"] in connection with John the Baptist, although he erroneously identifies John as a Christian!) The goal of "generative learning," for example, is reminiscent of Erikson's identification of generativity (vs. stagnation) as a crisis of mid-adulthood (Erikson's Stage 7) (Fowler, 1979, 52). With attention to generativity translated in the business world as "productivity," it is easy to understand how Senge's book could capture the imaginations of business types. But when Senge talks about an organization that does more than survive, that creates its future, he is talking about more than productivity.

Senge's learning organization also has characteristics Erikson identifies with "old age": integrity and wisdom (Erikson's Stage 8). The integrity of the organizational system, as in "systems thinking," corresponds to the ego-integrity of Erikson's old age. Managing (and expanding) the organization's capacity to create [Senge] corresponds to the older adult's wisdom. It involves a reasonable sense of one's place and abilities. As Fowler's "Erikson" says in his mythical symposium, it is the "acceptance of one's one and only life cycle" (Fowler, 1979, 86). As Thomas Groome says, summarizing Fowler,

> The stage six person dwells in the world as a transforming presence. . . . Life is both loved and held loosely; it is taken seriously, but not too seriously. (Groome, 1980, 69,73)

The point of all of this is to offer a challenge and vision to the church with respect to older adult ministries. The issue is not only how the church can recognize and honor older adults as continuing learners, but also how it can (re-)construct its life (and its educational systems) so that it does not simply repeat traditional activities, but creates new ones that foster and encourage continuing learning.

Examples of Continuing Older Adult Learning

Fortunately, this is not rocket science! It should not intimidate folk in local churches. Consider a few examples.

In my years of teaching in a local congregation, some of the most re-warding times have come when some of the older adults I have been working with have begun to connect and universalize. And the two functions are not so widely separate. The accumulation of experience is not always organized, but it calls for organization. Disconnected pieces of life challenge people to make sense of them, and making sense of them means relating them to a larger whole. To previous experience. To beliefs. To community norms. To a range of other "data." The particular both contributes to and also makes sense in light of the more universal.

How has this happened? My own practice has been to share *new* information with the older adults. In many congregations many older adults participate in a *Sunday School class* that employs a curriculum plan inaugurated in 1872 and now shepherded by the Committee on the Uniform Series of the National Council of Churches of Christ in the United States. This familiar three-year cycle of "uniform" lessons has been a mainstay of curriculum design for a number of denominations, and its use over time has resulted in a solid, if limited, Biblical literacy among older adults (a literacy lacking among church-goers of other generations!).

Now biblical literacy is one thing. "Putting it together" with other aspects of life is quite a different matter. My practice when working with adults with this experience has been to supplement their basic biblical (textual) literacy with observations and suggestions derived from other "liberal" studies, as well as the social sciences. Introducing "frames" or disciplines from economics, social anthropology or literature has often led to "aha!" moments, as the older students have discovered [more] exactly what a long-held practice does or looks like from another perspective. When it is *connected* to other parts of life (with which they also have experience) real learning, real re-creation, happens.

The work of Marcus Borg, for example, with its thorough-going insistence on setting the ministry of Jesus in the context of the "purity" system of first-century Judaism–an approach further amplified by the work of English social anthropologist Mary Douglas–has helped a number of older adults see their lifelong experience with some of the taboos of the church's popular social ethic ("I don't smoke and I don't chew and I don't go with girls that do") for what it is: a type of social formation not unlike that of other social [and religious] groups. Armed with such theoretical understanding, these older adults have then exercised their freedom to embrace and affirm, or criticize, these long-standing religious practices. Connecting them to a wider range of social experience, they are able to judge their appropriateness or inappropriateness with a sense of freedom and personal integrity. That does not mean class members have radically altered their lifestyles or abandoned long-practiced behaviors. Rather they have come to perceive their practices differently, and have endowed on them a legitimacy not because they are religious-grounded in the sense of dogmatically espoused, but because they truly function in a religious way–they tie life experiences together meaningfully (fr. *re-ligio*, to tie).

This offering of new framing information is the virtue of *elective church school classes* and *topical discussion groups* for older adults. But as just illustrated, the sensitive religious educator can also introduce such information in the context of traditional classes and programs. The key is to keep one's eyes on what helps older adults connect and universalize.

Connecting and universalizing remains a possibility for older adults through all three stages of older adulthood–active, transitional, frail. For the active senior, however, continued involvement in community activities is a particularly powerful way to continue learning. As time and energy allow, older adults can serve as *community volunteers*, bringing years of experience to emerging new problems. The conjunction of accumulated knowledge and a new situation offers the possibility that wisdom will emerge–wisdom that is more than the repetition of time-worn solutions or shibboleths, but the discovery of new "truth" for the day.

Connecting across even wider generational lines, old to young, can take place when older adults volunteer for *after-school programs* and *youth mentoring*. The key, again, is for the older adult *not* to simply assume that "age has its virtues," or all the answers, but that being older has given one the opportunity to face the challenge of dealing with new situations again and again. Older adults can help children and youth the most not by telling them what they've learned over the years, but showing them *how* they have learned over that same time.

Such problem solving is at the heart of the many *small business counseling corps* in which active older adults participate. Typically organized through a chamber of commerce, a business alliance, or perhaps a community college, these programs do not focus on religious education or spiritual development in a narrower sense, and it may seem a stretch to include them here. We certainly do not intend to suggest that older adults seek out such venues in order to express their religious convictions in an evangelical sense. Rather, we simply want to acknowledge that for many, the majority, in fact, vocation is realized in a career. Whether in a single job, or a series of them, a person labors both to establish his or her own livelihood, and to contribute to the good of the larger community. The knowledge and skills developed over a lifetime cannot simply be shut off at a particular age, even if one no longer labors for a salary. By helping others cope with the particular challenges they face, the older adult continues the stewardship of his or her "accumulated resources"–and usually also his or her learning.

One of the premiere examples of continuing older adult learning in Southern California can be seen in an organization called *Progressive Christians Uniting* (formerly, Mobilization for the Human Family). As its former title makes clear, the universalizing character of the organization is paramount. Although its new name underscores its *Christian* character, the organization has consistently taken up issues and concerns that impact a wide–indeed, global– spectrum of humanity: economics, politics, social ethics, etc. A collection of position papers was published in 2003 by a major Christian press.

What makes the PCU so interesting, however, is not simply that it addresses contemporary social and religious issues, but that its founder and prime mover is a 78-year-old emeritus professor of theology, John B. Cobb, Jr. Dr. Cobb's continuing engagement of a whole range of contemporary issues is both testimony and encouragement to continuing older adult learning.

Of course not everyone is equipped for such high-powered critical engagement, but everyone can be encouraged to continue learning. Groups focusing on resources such as Rabbi Shalomi-Schachter's *Ageing to Sage-ing* and James Birren's *Guided Autobiography* are designed to allow the individual older adult to tailor his or her continued learning to specific backgrounds and experiences. They invite the learner to rehearse his or her life, to identify significant events and pivotal moments, and to assess the meaning of them both personally and in connection with the larger community. The goal can be as simple as the construction of one's sense of personal legacy, or as complex as the engagement of contemporary social issues.

These are just some of the possibilities. As continuing learners, older adults themselves are continually coming up with new ideas. Persons working with them often simply need to provide support and encouragement.

CONCLUSION

In this chapter, we have argued that persons working with older adult ministries should have two important things in view: (1) the character of the older adult–whether active, transitional, or frail–as a lifelong, continuing learner; and (2) the opportunities (or, some would say, challenges) the church has to encourage and support the older adult as a learner.

The first point is supported by numerous psychosocial studies of adult development, as well as understandings of adult learning. The second, by past as well as emerging program ideas, as well as by the application to the church of Peter Senge's proposals for learning organizations.

NOTE

1. Such as those of Fowler, J. W. (1981). *Stages of Faith*. San Francisco: Harper and Row; Erikson, E. (1958). *Young Man Luther*. New York: Norton; *Erikson, E. (1963). Childhood and Society*. New York: Norton; Piaget, J. (1976). *The Child and Reality*. New York: Penguin; Kohlberg, L. (1976). *"Moral Stages and Moralization," Moral Development and Behavior*. New York: Holt, Rinehart, and Winston; Maslow, A. (1987). *Motivation and Personality* (3rd ed.). Boston: Addison-Wesley; Vaillant, G. (1977). *Adaptation to Life*. Boston: Little Brown; Levinson, D. (1978). *The Seasons of a Man's Life*. New York: Knopf; Gould, R. (1978). *Transformations: Growth and change in adult life*. New York: Simon & Schuster; Sheehy, G. (1976). *Passages: Predictable crises of adult life*. New York: Dutton.

REFERENCES

Compact Edition of the Oxford English dictionary, The. (1971). Oxford: Oxford University.

Fowler, J. (1979). Perspectives on the family from the standpoint of faith development theory. *The Perkins Journal*, 13-14.

Groome, T. (1980). *Christian religious education: Sharing our story and vision*. San Francisco: Harper & Row, 69, 73.

Knowles, M. (1980). *The modern practice of adult education: From pedagogy to andragogy*. Chicago: Associated Press, 43-62.

Roberts, D. B. (2000). What Constitutes Effective Teaching with Adults? In R. E. Reber & D. B. Roberts (Eds.), *A lifelong call to learn*. Nashville: Abingdon Press, 67-79.

Senge, P. M. (1990). *The fifth discipline: The art and practice of the learning organization*. New York: Doubleday.

Senge, P. M. (1994). *The fifth discipline field book: Strategies and tools for building a learning organization*. New York: Doubleday.

RECOMMENDED READINGS

Best, R. J., & Brunner, J. A. (1991). *I'll never forget our home, a healing guide for older people who choose to move forward to a new life*. Milwaukee: Montgomery Media, Inc.

Birren, J., & Cochran, K. (2001). *Telling the stories of life through guided autobiography groups*. Baltimore: Johns Hopkins Press.

Carlson, D. (1997). *Engaging in ministry with older adults*. Herndon: Alban Institute Publications.

Carroll, J. W., & Wade, C. R. (2002). *Bridging divided worlds: Generational cultures in congregations*. Indianapolis: Jossey-Bass Publishers.

Close, H. (2004). *Becoming a forgiving person: A pastoral perspective*. Binghamton: The The Haworth Press, Inc.

Cole, T., & Gadow, S. (Eds.). (1986). *What does it mean to grow old? Reflections from the humanities*. Durham: Duke University Press.

Frankl, V. (1959). *Man's search for meaning*. New York: Simon and Shuster.

Gaynor, A. (1999). *Images of God*. St. Paul: Hazeldon Press.

Guenther, M. (1992). *Holy listening: The art of spiritual direction*. Cambridge: Cowley Publications, 1.

Kimble, M., & McFadden, S. (2003). *Aging, spirituality, and religion: A handbook* (Vol. 2). Minneapolis: Fortress Press.

Kimble, M., McFadden, S., Ellor, J., & Seeber, J. (1995). *Aging, spirituality, and religion: A Handbook* (Vol. 1). Minneapolis: Fortress Press.

Miller, J. (1995). *Autumn wisdom: Finding meaning in life's later years*. Minneapolis: Augsburg Press.

Miller, J. (1995). *Winter grief, summer grace: Returning to life after a loved one dies*. Minneapolis: Augsburg Press.

Miller, J., & Cutshall, S. (2001). *The art of being a healing presence*. Fort Wayne: Willowgreen Publishing.

Morgan, R. (1996). *Remembering your story–A guide to spiritual autobiography*. Nashville: Upper Room Press.

Painter, C., & Valois, P. (1985). *Gifts of age*. San Francisco: Chronicle Books.

Schachter-Shalomi, Z. (1995). *From age-ing to sage-ing*. New York: Warner Books.

Seeber, J. (1990). *Spiritual maturity in later years*. Binghamton: The Haworth Press, Inc.

Tickle, P. (1995). *Re-discovering the sacred: Spirituality in America*. New York: Crossroad Publishing Company.

Spiritual Need Three:
Opportunities to Serve
"Call Me a Master, Not a *Senior* Citizen"

Bonnie Stover

SUMMARY. Human beings have a spiritual need to be involved in issues and people beyond themselves. Older Adults, with their education and experience, provide for a wealth of needs within a community. However, their conflict of time and interest often forms a barrier to serving. There are ways to avoid these barriers, and there are key messages that can encourage and support those who serve. Opportunities for older adults to serve are possible, no matter what their physical capabilities. Partnerships and collaborations with community organizations can make serving more effective and thus more pleasurable to everyone involved. *[Article copies available for a fee from The Haworth Document Delivery Service: 1-800-HAWORTH. E-mail address: <docdelivery@haworthpress. com> Website: <http://www.HaworthPress.com> © 2005 by The Haworth Press, Inc. All rights reserved.]*

KEYWORDS. Service, volunteers, roadblocks, spiritual, intergenerational programs, servant leadership

---

[Haworth co-indexing entry note]: "Spiritual Need Three: Opportunities to Serve 'Call Me a Master, Not a *Senior* Citizen.'" Stover, Bonnie. Co-published simultaneously in *Journal of Religion, Spirituality & Aging* (The Haworth Pastoral Press, an imprint of The Haworth Press, Inc.) Vol. 17, No. 3/4, 2005, pp. 87-95; and: *Ministering to Older Adults: The Building Blocks* (ed: Donald R. Koepke) The Haworth Pastoral Press, an imprint of The Haworth Press, Inc., 2005, pp. 87-95. Single or multiple copies of this article are available for a fee from The Haworth Document Delivery Service [1-800-HAWORTH, 9:00 a.m. - 5:00 p.m. (EST). E-mail address: docdelivery@haworthpress.com].

Available online at http://www.haworthpress.com/web/JRSA
2005 by The Haworth Press, Inc. All rights reserved.
doi:10.1300/J496v17n03_08

ONE OF THE ESSENTIAL SPIRITUAL NEEDS OF PEOPLE IS TO BE OF SERVICE

To engage the older adult population in service, we need to do a better job of understanding what is on their minds and what they might be looking for in new kinds of congregational and civic involvement. In other words, we need to ask them.

Part of the answer resides in creating more compelling opportunities for individuals to apply their energy and skills to service. For this generation of seniors, volunteering is much more than filling time. . . . It is about filling a need to both make a difference and be involved, says a researcher at Peter Hart Associates who wrote *The New Face of Retirement: An Ongoing Survey of American Attitudes on Aging.*[1]

Experience Counts

These committed, highly talented individuals are parlaying years of life-learning into inventive, unpaid positions. Scientists, teachers, firemen, executives are transforming what it means to grow old. A record number of fifty-pluses spend ten hours or more a week volunteering.

Retirement Can Be a Time of Conflicting Emotions

On one hand there is the feeling of exhilaration and a newfound sense of freedom. On the other hand there are the unsettling feelings of loneliness and loss of purpose, even for those who enjoy an active social life. They miss a particular kind of relationship–one linked to purposefulness. They miss the kind of relationships that were formed at work. They miss working together to solve problems, shared experiences throughout the day, and the camaraderie that came so naturally when purposes were linked.

Roadblocks to Service

While some older adults may be called to service by the simple urgency of the need, the majority are fiercely protective of their newfound freedom. They have fantasized about retirement as a time of idyllic pleasures and are prone to *distract* themselves from the void they feel. Frequently, such persons will say "it is time to give the young people a chance to help out" or simply proclaim how busy they are.

Avoiding the Roadblocks

No one at any age likes to think in terms of limitations. In particular, older adults do not appreciate statements suggesting that they don't have enough to do or that they are not useful anymore. They prefer to be acknowledged as credible, having accumulated years of wisdom and experience.

Finding the Appeal . . . What Do They Want?

- Control over their lives . . . not having to work for someone else is appealing to retirees. Service should not be perceived as compromising their sense of being in control of their own time.
- The idea of life as a journey with a future suggests a continuum–rather than a series of sections with beginnings, middles, and most of all *ends*.
- The idea of sharing what they have learned from experience and maturity.
- Being part of something larger to address social issues. The power of groups as agents of social change holds the promise of recreating purposeful relationships that many retirees miss so dearly.

Key Messages to Encourage Involvement

- Life is a continuing journey with never-ending opportunities to learn, give, and grow.
- New bridges are being built: from generation to generation, from skill to need, from interest to opportunity. We all need to be part of that process . . . no matter what our age, background or experience.
- Your experience, wisdom, and talents are needed and will be valued.
- Your freedom and autonomy will not be compromised.
- You know what you have to offer. We can help you find an outlet.
- Experiencing the unique satisfaction of "relationships with a purpose" need not be gone forever.

Church Leaders Can Expand Models to Meet Needs

When volunteers are included in setting the vision for their spiritual community, they are more willing to work towards reaching the goals. Involving volunteers from the beginning and getting their input is a big motivational factor in keeping volunteers positive and supportive of the congregational needs. Taking every opportunity to continue to keep people informed of changes/progress (through newsletters, meetings, and bulletins) makes it easier to stay involved. Connecting "present needs" to the "bigger picture" also allows volunteers to feel that they are part of attaining long term goals. For example, "envelope stuffers" in a fund raising drive need to know that the mailing they send out brings back the dollars needed to fund a special need.

It is critical that members of congregations *believe* that volunteer participation is an integral part of the church vision and is recognized by the leadership as an essential contribution toward reaching the goals of their spiritual community. Stereotypes still exist depicting the role of a church volunteer in predictable ways. It is important for church leadership to establish a mechanism that explores ongoing opportunities for volunteer involvement that sets a higher standard and raises the consciousness of the congregation to also see volunteers in skilled roles, as non-paid professional staff. Congregation members must be made aware how their skills and talents are needed to fill these roles and how that will benefit others.

It Takes a Village

Volunteering is spiritual by nature. Giving and receiving are part of the same circle. Those who give freely of their time and talents receive back tenfold, not the least of which is the satisfaction that comes with knowing that your efforts have helped someone else.

Since Congregations represent "spiritual community" for people of all ages, volunteer participation should be inclusive and involvement should be encouraged from every age group. When children are engaged in volunteer projects from an early age, they are more likely to mature into adults who associate volunteering with the progression of their spiritual growth. We all have a need to belong and when we understand that our contributions make a difference, it is very satisfying–no matter what our age or contribution.

Example

Intergenerational programs are a great way for congregations to work together to gain knowledge of and mutual respect for one another's talents and needs and to support the needs of the greater community. The following example shows how one congregation's intergenerational project worked:

A local foodbank was soliciting involvement from the community to support their efforts in providing food for needy families. A conversation with the foodbank director also revealed that the availability of "fresh" produce was nearly non-existent for their clients.

The church had an undeveloped lot on their property and decided to put out a call to the general membership to organize a steering committee to investigate the idea of planting a garden on the lot for the purpose of partnering with the food bank. The committee decided that it would be a good use for the property and an opportunity for their congregation to directly help their own needy families and also establish a community outreach project.

They divided the work into several categories with consideration for age groups and available resources. They asked the smallest children to participate by planting seeds in labeled cups. Those who were not able to take part in the physical tasks involved in preparing the lot and planting the garden were asked to take the "seeds in a cup" home and raise them for a few weeks, returning them when they reached a pre-determined maturation for planting in the garden.

In addition to vegetables, flower seeds were also planted in cups and taken to a local retirement community where seniors were asked to help nurture the seedlings. In return, members of the congregation agreed to bring flowers from the garden to the retirement community to be enjoyed by all the residents.

Over time the project became so well known throughout the entire community that other community groups, churches, and schools adopted the project, expanding participation to the development of several gardens. One of the gardens became a flower garden, with seniors from several retirement communities and congregations participating by nurturing seedlings.

Example

One congregation had to cut back on office staff leaving the pastor no choice but to route phone messages to a voice mail system when he was not available. To make the system more *people* friendly, the pastor coordinated a plan with one of the shut-in members of his congregation.

The pastor had the calls forwarded directly to his shut-in assistant during the time he was not available to answer the phones in person. Members of the congregation were much happier to hear the voice of a real person on the other end of the phone and his shut-in assistant was delighted to provide such a valuable service to the pastor and to the members of the congregation.

Think It Through/First Things First

Identifying needs is paramount to the success of any volunteer effort. Too often the best intentions miss the mark because we impose our own ideas of what "doing good" should be, without researching the facts first. Too often people are disappointed with the outcome of an effort when "how will we measure our success" was not part of the planning process.

Example

Two-hundred fresh turkeys, donated specifically for the homeless, were dropped off at the social services department at the county hospital one Christmas. The staff had to call the donors to come back and pick up the turkeys.

- The hospital had no facilities to refrigerate 200 turkeys. They would spoil rapidly.
- The staff had no way to contact 200 homeless families. The homeless don't have phones and rarely do they have transportation.
- The homeless have no way to cook a turkey.

The donors were disappointed when their turkeys could not be accepted but understood why and were redirected in a way that their efforts could support their goal.

The hospital staff redirected the donors to the nearest homeless shelter where there were facilities to store, prepare, and serve the turkeys. The shelter was a place where homeless families knew they could come for a holiday meal.

Partnering and Collaboration

Sometimes it just makes sense to partner/collaborate with others. And identifying and meeting the needs of the aging population might best be served by collaborating with a network of organizations that have something in common with your purpose. Organizations who are working towards similar goals can make great partners.

Example

The "Healthy City Initiative" brought people together in the City of Glendale in a way that had not been done before. They formed a "Healthy City Coalition"; a grassroots effort of over seventy-five individuals and groups representing churches, hospitals, businesses, media, schools, social service agencies, police and fire departments, and city government. The goal was to make Glendale a "Healthy City" in every way for all residents.

The Coalition began its efforts with a comprehensive (citywide) Needs Assessment. Once needs were identified, smaller coalitions formed to find solutions for the specific areas of identified need. Here are just some of their results:

- A homeless shelter was opened in Glendale featuring a health clinic supplied and staffed by the three area community hospitals. The shelter was also staffed with representatives from community social service agencies and churches. The Salvation Army provided meals. The goal was to offer all services under one roof that could support the transition of the homeless into permanent housing and jobs.
- Teams of medical, social service, and parish nurses assessed homebound seniors and shut-ins. Community resources were mobilized depending on individual needs. The parish nurses became an integral part of assessment teams and a link to broader resources in the medical, social service, and spiritual community.
- Senior centers and church congregations were targeted for health fairs, nutritional and medication counseling, and wellness education.
- "Healthy Kids" mobilized resources for children not covered by medical/dental insurance (identified in the schools). They received assessments and follow-up for needed medical, vision, and/or dental services. The three community hospitals agreed to underwrite the cost of surgery for these children, too.
- Community churches/organizations/food banks, etc., offering free or low-cost support services, worked together to coordinate their efforts, reducing service gaps. Eventually a comprehensive list of

available services was published, circulated, and posted through-out the community and in the local newspaper.

- Retired teachers and professionals were recruited and trained to volunteer in a phone bank for "latchkey" kids. Children could call in on a toll free number to get help with homework or just to talk to someone if they became lonely or afraid until their parents came home from work. Program information packets and phone decals were distributed through the churches and schools. One child's life was saved when he called to report that his brother was playing with a gun. The well-trained volunteer knew just what to do to keep the child on the line while she alerted the police who arrived in time.

- Grief and loss facilitator training was offered by a community pro-fessional at no charge to the lay ministry of local churches if they would form groups in their own congregations. The training also included issues of loss related to aging.

SERVANT LEADERS

Call Me a Master, Not a Senior Citizen

Motivation of others is a primary skill of seasoned servant-leaders. They make sure that individuals tap into one (or more) of three domi-nant motivations: Affiliation, Achievement, and Power. *Affiliation* builds effective teams so individuals can bond with others. *Achieve-ment* gives people goals to reach for, and *Power* puts people in charge and recognizes them for getting the job done. Individuals are the most motivated when they know the work is challenging, have the sense they are achieving something of value, are given increased responsi-bility that supports their growth and development, and receive recog-nition for their accomplishments. It is critical that leaders find ways to convey the significance of even the most basic effort to the overall goal and mission of the organization.

NOTE

1. Results of a survey conducted by Peter D. Hart Research Associates, August, 2002. Published on Civic Ventures Website: civicventure.org

RECOMMENDED READING

Ellis, S. J. (1996). *From the top down* (2nd ed.). Philadelphia: Energize, Inc.

Unknown. (2004). *Volunteer leadership series (group's volunteer leadership series).* Loveland: Group Publishing.

Volunteer Management Report, The. Published monthly by Stevenson, Inc. Phone 712-239-3010 or visit www.stevensoninc.com

Wittich, B. (2000). *The care and feeding of volunteers.* Fullerton: Knowledge Transfer Publishing.

Spiritual Need Four:
Opportunities to Be Served
and to Share with Others

Donald R. Koepke, MDiv, BCC
James Ellor, DMin, PhD

SUMMARY. Older adults have unique opportunities to be served and to share with others through groups and individual relationships and programs in religious congregations. Where programs and senior centers with public funding can provide only for physical, emotional, and social needs, religious congregations can be more wholistic and provide for the spiritual needs as well. This chapter offers further discussion of planning that will facilitate program development for the whole person. *[Article copies available for a fee from The Haworth Document Delivery Service: 1-800-HAWORTH. E-mail address: <docdelivery@haworthpress.com> Website: <http://www.HaworthPress.com> © 2005 by The Haworth Press, Inc. All rights reserved.]*

KEYWORDS. Wholistic, spiritual, spirituality, geist, planning, frail elderly, soul, assessment tool, needs-based programming

---

[Haworth co-indexing entry note]: "Spiritual Need Four: Opportunities to Be Served and to Share with Others." Koepke, Donald R., and James Ellor. Co-published simultaneously in *Journal of Religion, Spirituality & Aging* (The Haworth Pastoral Press, an imprint of The Haworth Press, Inc.) Vol. 17, No. 3/4, 2005, pp. 97-119; and: *Ministering to Older Adults: The Building Blocks* (ed: Donald R. Koepke) The Haworth Pastoral Press, an imprint of The Haworth Press, Inc., 2005, pp. 97-119. Single or multiple copies of this article are available for a fee from The Haworth Document Delivery Service [1-800-HAWORTH, 9:00 a.m. - 5:00 p.m. (EST). E-mail address: docdelivery@haworthpress.com].

Available online at http://www.haworthpress.com/web/JRSA
© 2005 by The Haworth Press, Inc. All rights reserved.
doi:10.1300/J496v17n03_09

Providing services for the elderly is the most common form of Older Adult Ministry found within faith communities (Tobin et al., 1986). This focus is fueled by the medicalization of aging where culture describes "old" as being frail, inadequate, and needy. While this book has sought to broaden the perspective that OAMs are a ministry to and with the frail, many congregations still believe that Older Adult Ministry is primarily a ministry to the frail.

Americans are living longer and healthier. In 1900 the average life span for persons in the United States was around 46 years. Today that average has soared to 77.11 years (Gelfand, 2003, xiv). Modern medicine, diet, access to clean water, indoor plumbing and more, has all contributed to these extra years. But these advances are not without cost. People may live longer and healthier, but the longer they live, they will also need to learn to live with chronic illness. In the beginning of the 20th century people died within four days of contracting the illness that finally took their life. Today seniors are more likely to die from multisystems failure, each of which, at the point of death, is being treated by a physician. The result is that people "slide out" rather than "drop out" of life, providing a longer period of slow decline and ill health.

That people live longer, healthier while at the same time are sick longer has a significant impact on ministry. People are seeking to remain in their homes longer. Community resources have been developed that encourage this desire and make its fulfillment possible. The result is that there are more people in faith communities who have more physical, psychological, social, and spiritual needs than ever. At one time, informal clustering of persons within a faith community had the capability to handle the needs of their elders. Today, because of the sheer numbers of older adults in a community, those informal structures, while remaining valuable, are not adequate to provide the depth and breadth of services that are needed. Some members of a faith group are "well-connected" within a congregational community. For example, when the spouse of the choir director dies, one can watch the concern for the bereaved come pouring forth. But many others are not so connected and can easily slip through the cracks. The result is that the informal caring that faith communities have long cherished needs to become organized and intentional. Most faith communities embrace the call to provide for the most vulnerable among them, widows and orphans, or the New Testament call to cloth the naked and feed the hungry (Matthew, 25).

THE STRUGGLE WITH DEPENDENCY

There remains an additional reason for providing service to others within a faith community: the spiritual health of the individual person who is in need. We live in a society that prides itself on being independent, self-assured, and capable. The day when a youngster can "go potty in the big potty" becomes a day of celebration for child and parent alike. We savor receiving our driver's license and anxiously await the day when we own our first car. We feel complete and adequate when able to live independently from parents, choose our own life-mates, and simply "make it" on our own. To become dependent on anyone or anything is to experience the depths of negation as a human person. Many older adults cling to their independence with the tenacity of a bulldog.

Faith communities share in a vision that human beings are inter-dependent. The traditions of both Christianity and Judaism suggest that the shedding of ego and the embrace of being connected-beyond-the-self is the height of human experience. "Don't put your trust in princes or the things of the earth" (Psalm: 146). "If anyone would come after me, let him deny himself, take up his cross and follow me" (Mark, 8). Highfield and Cason, in an issue of the 1983 journal *Cancer Nursing*, suggest that one of four basic spiritual needs of persons is to be able to "receive love" not just "give love" (Highfield, 1983, 188). It is a call for the embrace of our own need and for the receiving of gifts from beyond ourselves and personal strength. It is a call for inter-dependency. Thus, the spiritual challenge for faith communities is to provide opportunities for persons to be served–to let down their defenses, swallow their pride, and enter a relationship of interdependence with open hands, not only to give but to receive.

Opportunities to be served have long been at the forefront of congregational culture in the United States. Many, if not most, faith communities characterize themselves as a "family" who takes care of each other. Historically, these acts of caring have taken the form of telephone assurance programs, delivery of flowers to the home-centered, special visitation both at home and hospital, food pantries, and transportation services, to name but a few. It is an easy step to an OAM that provides opportunities to be served. Faith communities have been providing such supports for years. With the increased number of older adults living longer and healthier but also living longer sicker the challenge is for planning to become more focused and intentional so that a faith community might not only do good, but do good well.[1]

INCLUDING THE SPIRITUAL IN THE PLANNING

In his chapter on the spirituality of the Eagle Clan Mother, Drew Leader (1997, 101) shares the story of an elderly woman who is a key spiritual leader in the Onondaga nation. Eagle Clan Mother shares that in her tradition the spiritual leader is selected from among the elders of the tribe based on their observations of the life she has lived and the way she has cared for her family. While this person is often the oldest woman in the tribe, this is not always the case. In the discussion of her role, she speaks of being concerned for the life lived by each person, his or her feelings, physical needs, social relationships, and the nature of his or her relationship with the spirit. In this way, the Eagle Clan Mother has reflected common elements of what seems to be understood as the *spiritual*. First, she reflects that the spiritual seems to reflect *transcendence* and second it is what can be called *wholistic*. While these are not her terms, they begin to position the discussion in the larger context. It is challenging to talk about developing programs that meet the spiritual needs of older adults, if one is not sure what a spiritual need is.

The literature is filled with a wide variety of meanings of this term *spirituality*. Yet, there is also no clear universal definition. Some of the confusion stems from its origins. The words spiritual or spirituality are well known in the mystical elements of the Jewish and Roman Catholic traditions and clearly understood in such eastern traditions as Buddhism and Hinduism. However, most of the Protestant traditions have little or no basis for familiarity with it. Within Protestant Christian nomenclatures, such terms as the *soul* or the *Holy Spirit* are better understood, yet still not universally defined. If only John Calvin, Martin Luther, or John Wesley had discussed *spirituality* in the way it is currently being used, there would be wider Protestant insight. However, until this term became more popular in the 1970s and 1980s many Protestants were unfamiliar with it, at least in the context of their own faith traditions.

Confusion is also found in the academic arena. Walter Wili notes, "The psychologist of the old school took little interest in the 'spirit'" (Wili, 1954, 75). He explains that it seemed to be entirely too supernatural. Thus, writers in the humanities, social sciences, and philosophy were more comfortable with it. While this has continued to be true in some circles, there are clear exceptions. Carl Jung and Viktor Frankl, among the great thinkers in psychology, and notables such as Paul Tillich in theology have addressed and in some cases embraced these terms.

For the academic, the term has been seen as the more *politically correct* approach to discuss issues of religion. In Gerontological circles this becomes clear in the study of the various topics deemed important for discussion at the White House Conferences on Aging. In 1961, there was a section on Religion, but for the 1971 White House Conference on Aging, this term was seen as controversial, so according to Arthur Flemming (Flemming, 1995), Clark Tibbitts and his planning team manufactured the term *Spiritual Well-being*. While this term employs the word *spiritual*, it is built on the 1960s concept of psychological well-being, which creates even more confusion. However, it offered an approach to religion and spirituality that seemed to be seen as less denominationally driven and more acceptable in inter-faith circles.

Possibly the only safe conclusion is that there are many different voices who are defining this term with very little agreement as to the definition, or even philosophical or theological basis for the term. It has been observed in many different professional meetings that there are simply two key distinctions. First, spirituality is probably a part of religion, but it may not be. Religion seems to reflect the dogmas and institutional structures of the church, synagogue, and temple. Second, spirituality is understood to be highly personal, reflecting a personal relationship for some with a higher power, for some with nature, or for some a combination of the two. Many Christian clergy would like to think that these two are compatible but there is not universal agreement on this point.

So how then should a congregation interested in addressing more than the psychosocial needs of seniors begin to think about the spiritual needs? One suburban Presbyterian church did a needs assessment of their congregation. Among the needs on the list were day care, after school programs, youth groups, senior citizen clubs, and at the end, someone added spiritual growth. The option was not any better defined than that, but it was the most commonly selected with 60 percent requesting more help with their spirituality. The next nearest concern had only a 22 percent response. The quandary for the congregational leadership was *what does this mean?* Sixty percent of those filling out the questionnaire had asked them to offer more programming that addressed spiritual needs, but no one seemed to know what this meant. In this case, they responded by not responding to it.

The first task of any congregational planning group then is to come to some understanding of what is meant by the spiritual needs of the congregation. Is it a form of growth in faith, spiritual formation, or Biblical reflection? It may be elements of all three. The task of the planning committee will be to create a common vision (Worley, 1978). According to Worley, a common planning vision is a simple, well-articulated statement that all on the planning group can agree to, that describes the goals of the program. Described elsewhere in this volume as a mission statement, this key ingredient helps planners to be sure that they are all on the same page. However, getting there is a critical part of the journey.

Most often when older adults talk about spiritual needs, what they seem to be looking for is a greater sense of closeness to *that which is greater than we are.* For some this is a euphemism for God, for others it is more of a need to be closer to creation and may or may not include God. However it is understood, it may be helpful to think about this task in several ways. The following table suggests that there are at least five ways to operationalize this task. Few congregations will find all of these approaches to be useful. In fact, none of them may work for some congregations. However, in order to start the discussion, they offer five initial themes. What all five have in common reflects the discussion of the Eagle Clan Mother. First and foremost, each reflects some type of transcendence. In the German theological tradition the root word for spirit is *Geist.* In German, it depends on which suffix one puts on it as to whether it means spirit in relation to the Divine (God) or in relationship to other human beings. The latter is often referred to in psychology as self-transcendence and is sometimes inadequately measured by reflections of social skills. In some ways, it seems artificial to separate transcendence into interpersonal relationship and relationships with God, but this particular system followed by Paul Tillich and others allows for discussions of the *human spirit* and *God's spirit* or the *Holy Spirit.* It is this system that is employed by existentialists such as Viktor Frankl to understand the nature of *meaning.*

	Mystical Relationship with Nature	Traditional Bible Study or Prayer Group	Spiritual Formation	Individual Relationship with the Divine	Faith Development
Individual					
Group					

When the development of a spiritual relationship is mentioned, it is often in the context of the search for meaning in the life of the person. Meaning in this context becomes the human ramification or benefit of a quality spiritual relationship with God. In other words, by finding a deeper spiritual relationship, one finds meaning in life. While the two can be separate, they have in common this concept of transcendence. Most existentialists would agree that one cannot find either a spiritual relationship or inner meaning without first finding some sort of transcendence. What that means functionally for programs is that when a senior is beginning a search for meaning, direct them first to find ways to express transcendence or giving on themselves. Churches are easy places to find such outlets. Depending on the gifts of the individual involved, having him or her lead a Bible study, visit the sick, or any number of necessary ministry tasks, including sweeping out the children's playroom, can offer this sense of transcendence, meaning, and purpose. Meaning, like spirituality, is defined by the individual who is on the journey, not necessarily by clergy or dogmas or public opinion. It is critical to understand that the search for spiritual connection and/or meaning is not necessarily dependent on a visit to a monastery on a hilltop, or a long walk in a very hot desert. Anything that puts people in the position to be able to give to others can offer meaning to some persons.

The second common ingredient is that of wholism. Granger Westburg first employed this term in the 1960s to refer to a holism that is more than the understanding that the physical, social, and emotional self are all one person and cannot be separated. Too often the wisdom of Alfred Adler has been understood to reflect the three basic human elements to the exclusion of the spiritual. It is true, as Adler notes, that if you cut off a leg, the person will also have feelings about it. These two cannot be separated. It will also impact the person's spiritual self. Thus, Westburg added the *W* and is credited by most with bringing the spelling Wholism into modern nomenclature. Spirituality is always wholistic. It is generally felt that one cannot simply extract the spiritual in the way that Peter Pan could somehow lose his shadow. Rather, the spiritual permeates all aspects of the person.

From these two common elements of *transcendence* and *wholism* we can come back to the five approaches to understand how to work with the spiritual. The first reflects a *Mystical Relationship with Nature*. This is relationship with God's creation for some people, but for a Buddhist and others there need not be a relationship to the Divine. However this is understood, it generally reflects a need to be closer to nature, to mother earth. Thus, programs that reflect nature, creation, and the world around us would all fit into this group. Keeping in mind that this relationship is mystical, it may not be easily catalogued or pressed into some sort of programmatic template. Sometimes it is more a matter of making things available to persons interested in this, such as nature walks in local parks, or a trip to the mountains, or a ride on a boat. At other times, it may involve retreats to retreat centers for more meditative activities. It will simply need to reflect all of the creativity of those involved.

The second theme reflects the *Traditional Bible Study or Prayer Group*. Christian churches have done this for centuries. In some congregations this may also include study of other traditional texts that reflect their own understanding of faith, but in any case these are groups that are clearly present in most religious groups.[2] For many, these first two categories will include the next three. However, for others, there may be a deeper meaning in them.

The third theme helps provide focus for those interested in *Spiritual Formation*. There are many different ways to obtain this. In some contexts, spiritual formation is operationalized much like going to a counselor, except that the task is spiritual care, rather than emotional support. Thus, at appropriate intervals, such as once a week, the senior would visit their spiritual advisor for an hour. Others participate in groups or covenantal communities working together to seek spiritual formation. These may involve Bible study, prayer, and meditation as well as dialogue with others. In some religious traditions spiritual formation is an established part of individual and even professional growth for clergy.

Focus on the *Individual's Own Relationship with the Divine or God* is a fourth theme. This is not one approach, but as many as there are people seeking to enhance their own spiritual experience. To understand the individual relationship with God is to comprehend the fullness of one's own spiritual life in relationship with all that surrounds us that is of God. It is entirely built on the perception of the individual. Thus to program for this relationship is to try to understand from each person what is understood and needed.

Finally, *Faith Development* is a thematic approach developed by several authors including James Fowler (Fowler, 1995). Faith development parallels human development in that it suggests there are developmental steps or stages which a person goes through. Fowler and others work to disentangle this parallel, however, as there is effort to not suggest that some stages are somehow superior or more important than others. Rather, the stages help to develop the individual in various ways. Faith development starts by assuming a subject-to-object relationship or a relationship between the person and God. Without God, or without the person, there can be little discussion of faith. As such then, this approach includes reflection on this relationship in whatever form is helpful to the individual or group involved. It may involve discussion groups on knowing God; it may reflect meditations on the impact of God in one's life; it may involve a strengthening of prayer. In any case, it is understood as a journey or process that moves from one place in development to another.

There are many voices that are holding up the need for spirituality and spiritual growth. Only a subjective evaluation would suggest which one is best or right for any individual or group. The journey to develop such programs must begin by listening to those primarily involved. Religious congregations are in a unique position to offer this sort of service. Publicly funded programs for seniors cannot do so. If we are going to argue wholistically that the spiritual is a vital part of the nature of the person, then it is as important to provide spiritual programs and services as it is to provide meals, medical care, or transportation. Wholism would suggest that both are needed and critical to the well-being of older adults.

IN PLANNING, DON'T FORGET THE RECIPIENTS

As with other aspects of Older Adult Ministry, it is essential to include those who will be receiving care in the planning for care. All too often a well-meaning, well-intentioned planning group puts hours into developing a service which they feel is essential to the needs of the frail and transitional elders in their community. The problem comes when they construct a lemonade stand when the people they are seeking to serve desire orange juice. Frail and transitional adults can be included in the planning process in several ways.

1. Hold planning meetings in the home of the frail/transitional adult. Many frail and transitional persons are sharp verbally and cognitively but their legs, or their sight, might limit their ability to gather outside their own home. Ask other members of the group to provide the required coffee and munchies. Meet at a time of day when the older adult can more readily participate. Try meeting during the day. A daytime meeting would limit who could participate in the planning process to people who are available during the day (older adults), which might be an advantage.
2. Include the frail and the transitional in a telephone conference call with the entire committee. These calls, for a price, are easily organized through any telephone carrier. Some congregations have the capability of "conference calling" on their telephone system that

would allow the planning group to confer with a frail/transitional person at no additional cost. Major programmatic sections of national conventions have been planned solely by means of telephone conference calls.

IDENTIFYING THE NEED

Another way of including the receivers of congregational services is to conduct a needs assessment survey. The appendix of this book contains a simple, easy to use, assessment form that can be duplicated and used as is or adapted to local settings and resources. A word of caution: it is always important to remember that any form taken from any source, including this one, needs to be reviewed by local people to make sure that the service needs being assessed are service needs that are capable of being delivered. There is nothing worse than for a frail older adult to declare a need that cannot or will not be fulfilled. Using the list of existing older adult ministries from Part One, Chapter Three of this book can assist in adapting the needs survey to the local situation and capabilities.

Note that the survey in the appendix assesses all needs, be they physical, emotional or spiritual, from a spiritual point of view, or at least from a participation-in-religious-activities perspective. All too often the focus of ministries that provide opportunities to be served focuses only on what can be seen, touched, tasted, heard, or proved. While these concerns of the body are tangible and a felt need from a recipient point of view, a faith community needs to be focused on more than physical and emotional well-being. Faith communities need to address physical and emotional issues from a spiritual, or at least a congregational participation perspective. "Why are we doing this program?" is an important question to ask. Keep your mission statement (Part One, Chapter Two) at the forefront of the planning process since it is easy to become just another social service organization. While this mission is okay on its surface, it is only part of a congregation's mission.

How the survey is conducted is also important. Instead of mailing out a written survey that is easily set aside and forgotten or even ignored, what about conducting a telephone survey, or better yet, a personal visit to each frail/transitional person by a pair of planning group members. Such personal attention will not only increase participation in the survey, but allow planning group members to really know their audience. If a telephone survey is planned, consider recruiting frail/transitional persons to share in the phoning, providing them the opportunity to serve as well as to be served.

USING THE ASSESSMENT TOOL

The tool is divided into five sections based upon four spiritual needs. First, spiritually speaking, a person needs a sense of belonging to something outside of herself or himself. These are relationships that a person can experience with the senses. A second spiritual need is to have a connection with God, whom they cannot see. A third spiritual need is to "continue learning and growing," a sense of future, and a belief that change is not loss but adventure. It involves being willing to grow as a person and is one of the hallmarks of "successful" aging. Spiritual need four, "doubts and struggles," is based upon a belief that spiritual growth always comes through struggle and even pain (sometimes). A person can have difficulty seeing "God" in the changes and losses that can accompany aging unless they have a creative understanding and experience of the role of suffering and struggle in spiritual growth. Finally, "hindrances" gives persons the opportunity to express that which gets in the way of their participation in the church family (and struggles with God?) by means of a simple check-off list. A number of responses declaring difficulty with vision, for example, might lead a planning committee to place a shade on the window that is behind the pulpit or duplicate worship materials in larger print, or increase the intensity of the lighting in the worship center. "I can't remember names" could be an indicator of dementia that might signal the need for further assessment. "Lost interest in being among people" could flag depression. "Personal issues" might raise an incontinence problem that might encourage a physical fitness class that has incontinence assistance as a component (there are physical fitness strategies that help address incontinence problems). "No Friends" might indicate the need for community building.

Upon reviewing an early version of this assessment form, one person responded,

> In my opinion, I wouldn't even make the option of doing it over the phone unless distance was a problem. Body language is just too important to me. Also, assessing some of the surroundings in the home and gives an opportunity to identify possible needs there.

Two, thoughts on what hinders me. . . . Once visiting a elder member of our congregation, I found out, with MUCH sweetness and encouragement, that he wasn't attending church because he no longer tithed. For his generation and culture THAT was a source of embarrassment. I learned a lot that day. Also, I have been told that older members avoid church because they are embarrassed to walk up to communion with a cane, walker or worse a wheelchair. When offered communion at their seat, many will say no because they don't what to attract attention, another midwest, stubborn Lutheran thing. Some have loosened up and we redid the sanctuary so that there are no more steps to receive communion.[3]

As the survey is administered, it is important to realize that not all seniors are alike. Life experiences, education, expanding values, even changes in religious perspectives make older adults less homogenous than at any time in their lives. Face-to-face conversation between two human beings will always be more effective that other methods, even if they are easier and quicker to administer. Many older persons are reluctant to participate in a survey that asks "personal" questions about values and beliefs regarding aging. In these cases the ministry doesn't just happen when the program is implemented. The ministry with older adults can begin with the planning process itself.

THE USE OF COMMUNITY RESOURCES IN CONGREGATIONAL MINISTRY

With needs so varied and complex, many congregations discover that they neither have the time, the staff–paid or volunteer–nor the finances to provide adequately for the needs of the transitional and frail in their midst. For example, sometimes a congregation is blessed with a person with the needed skills and thus is able to establish a much needed caregiver support group. Other congregations, because of size, have the capability to have a parish nurse or even a pastoral counselor on staff. But often, appropriate resources are not available in the congregation and so they need to be found in the local community.

Five Levels of Interaction

Sheldon Tobin et al., in the book *Enabling the Elderly: Religious Institutions within the Community Service System*, describe five levels of interaction between congregation and community organization that can lead to improved programming for both organizations (Tobin et al., 1986, 149).

The first is *communication*, which can be verbal, written, or any other form of communication. This form of interaction is usually limited to sharing information or ideas between organizations and includes consultation. Information about how to begin a hot lunch program for seniors could be secured from a community organization that provides that service in another area. Results of the Needs Survey could be shared with the local Area Agency on Aging, adding perhaps to their own resources and planning for the future. In communication, there is a transfer of information only. Both congregation and community organization retain independence.

A second form of interaction is *cooperation*. This form is when two or more separate organizations plan and implement independent programs but work toward similar, non-conflicting goals. The organizations share information but act on it independently. Organizations advertise for each other and try to avoid unnecessary duplication of services.

Coordination takes place when two or more organizations not only cooperate in planning and implementation of separate programs, but efforts are made to insure smooth interaction between these separate programs, avoid conflict, waste, or unnecessary duplication. Organizations that coordinate services not only share information and advertise for one another, but referrals are made to each program by the other. Thus a congregation may choose to open an adult day care center and receive referrals and marketing help from the local senior center, community care managers, or counseling office. At the same time, persons identified as having needs that can be met by the local senior center would be referred by the congregation to the senior center. While still independent, congregation and community organization increase their interaction and dependency on the other.

Collaboration is where two or more separate organizations join together to provide a single program or service. Each organization maintains its own identity but resources are jointly shared. Sometimes this collaboration results in the forming of a separate corporation with its own board of directors, budget and staff. Many a community "food pantry" is the result of several congregations collaborating together with community organizations, even local government. Congregations have often provided the needed space for community organizations to offer service not only to members of that faith community, but also to neighborhood residents.

The final level of interaction between congregation and community organization noted in *Enabling the Elderly* is *confederation*. This form is seldom used except when either congregation or community organization is "going out of business" and their resources become available to the partner. Confederation is when two or more organizations merge to promote programs or services. None of the participating organizations maintain a separate identity or separate resources. In the early 1990s a congregation in Long Beach, California, disbanded and gave their property to the local Lutheran Social Services agency, who continue to use the campus for an extensive community outreach program that includes not only emergency food and clothing, but also English as a second language, child care, and budgeting classes.

Using the Levels of Interaction

This discussion is given in order to encourage congregational leaders and older adult program planners to use community organizations as a vital resource in the development of their own ministry. Too often, faith communities have a "go-it-alone" mentality that suggests that if the church doesn't directly provide a service, then the service is not a function of the congregation. How many congregations have members who are underserved just because "they do not have the time, staff, and money for the ministry?" Such services could be provided by groups outside the congregation without threatening the values and beliefs of the congregation.

Often, community organizations would welcome cooperative and/or collaborative services with a congregation. A caregiver resource center could provide a trained support group leader while the congregation provides a comfortable and safe location. Information about a care-management seminar at the local senior center could be listed in a congregational worship bulletin. Following is a listing of national organizations that provide direct service, information, and education to any community group, including churches, free of charge. A simple "white page" telephone book search could result in an extended ministry being formed to the transitional and frail within any faith community . . . free.

Community Resources for Congregational Ministry

One obvious organization is the Alzheimer's Association (800-272-3900 or *www.alz.org*). Cooperation or collaboration with this organization can provide speakers for groups of older adults, support groups for caregivers, legal assistance, a 24-hour helpline (often in multi-languages), home care assistance, professional education and educational events, even a library on one of the most feared experiences of aging. Local offices of The Alzheimer's Association can be found on this Website by entering a zip code.

The National Council on Aging (800-373-4906 *www.ncoa.org*) has a vast array of services that can be used in congregational ministry. One is the Benefits Checkup (*www.benefitscheckup.org*) and Benefits Checkup Rx (*www.benefitscheckuprx.org*). Using the congregation's office computers with Web-access on weekends or Sundays, congregations can provide older adults with the latest government benefits for which they are eligible. A guided, step-by-step process, that takes about 15 minutes to perform, can result in significant savings on drugs as well as other federal and state benefits.

Many older adults have legal questions surrounding not only finances but also matters of health, life, and death. A local probate attorney might be willing to provide educational events in issues such as Living Trusts, wills, durable power of attorney for financial matters, durable power of attorney for health care, and the like. The National Academy of Elder Law Attorneys (*www.naela.org*) provides referrals to elder law attorneys using zip codes.

Although it might have a different name in a specific community, every county in America has an Area Agency on Aging (*www.aoa.dhhs.gov*). By searching for your community by name or zip code, a congregation can get in touch with all of the federal resources that are available. One of these resources of the Office on Aging is the ombudsman program that visits long term care communities in each community as an advocate for the resident, not the facility. One of the many items that these volunteers are trained to seek is signs of elder abuse in these facilities. Every county also has an Adult Protective Services organization as a part of county government. These persons can provide a wealth of information and consultation regarding abuse of the transitional and frail elderly living in the community rather than a facility.

Another Area Office on Aging service provided every county in America is HICAP, the Health Insurance Counseling and Advocacy Program. Funded by federal dollars, this volunteer program provides free counseling and educational services to older adults and their families. They posses the most current information designed to help people find their way through the maze of health insurance regulations and coverage. Working with a HICAP counselor you will get unbiased information to help you make the best choices for your individual health care needs because a HICAP counselor cannot sell, endorse, or recommend any specific insurance. What HICAP can do is help you understand:

- Your rights as a health care consumer
- Your Medicare benefits and rights, including how to appeal a Medicare claim denial
- Medicare and health insurance jargon
- Private Medicare supplemental health insurance policy benefits and exclusions
- HMOs and how they work
- Long-term-care insurance

The means of contacting this free service can be accessed through the Area Office on Aging Website, *www.aoa.dhhs.gov.*

What if a congregation's needs assessment reveals issues surrounding housing. What is the difference between a skilled nursing facility, an assisted living facility, and adult day care? When should a family consider hospice? Check with a local long-term-care community, or retirement community, in your area. Make a request for one of their staff to meet with the older adults in your congregation and/or their caregivers to discuss options. While a congregation might have to endure something of a sales pitch for their community, the information that they will share can be invaluable. The American Association of Homes and Services for the Aging (*www.ashsa.org*) has publications and information regarding not-for-profit retirement communities in virtually every city in the nation.

The support of caregivers can be an essential ministry of a congregation. Helping those who are helping the transitional and the frail speaks to the heart of congregational self-image. The National Alliance for Caregiving (*www.caregiving.org*) has wonderful resources for the family caregiver. Names and addresses of local sources of respite care, online support groups using secure lines, information on long-distance caregiving, tips for caregiving survival, and more are on this site. A small-group leader could easily develop resources for "support of caregivers" even just from the resources to be gained here.

Sometimes it can be helpful for an individual family to confer with a professional care manager who is acquainted not only with needs but community resources to fill those needs. Many care managers would be willing to present to groups small and large on local resources that can help in the caregiving task. A local caregiver can be found through the National Association of Professional Geriatric Care Managers (*www.caremanager.org*) just by entering a zip code.

What if the need is to provide services within the home? More and more people are living at home with needs that 15 years ago would have placed them in an institution. Again, resources for individual consultation as well as group educational presentations can be secured through local home care agencies. The name and phone number of these local agencies can be accessed through the state chapters of The National Association of Home Care (*www.nahc.org*).

Any survey of community resources cannot ignore the long-term work of the many disease-specific organizations: The American Heart Association (*www.americanheart.org*), the American Stroke Association (*www.strokeassociation.org*), the American Diabetes Association (*www.diabetes.org*), the National Multiple Sclerosis Society (*www.nmss.org*), the ALS Association (*www.alsa.org*), and the National Parkinson's Foundation (*www.parkinson.org*) have long been leaders for information and support for persons. Just making these sites available to members of your faith community can provide a significant service to them.

Community Organizations Can Provide Resources and Context for Congregational Ministry

The poet John Donne wrote: "No man is an island, entire of itself" (in Meditation XVIII, from *Devotions Upon Emergent Occasions* (1624)). Unfortunately, local faith groups often act as though they are an island to themselves. If a program doesn't have their denominational stamp on it, or if members of their community are not part of the planning process, faith groups are often absent from vital organizations. Local faith organizations can receive professional expertise, education, and consultation for their ministry by simply joining national organizations holding a similar vision of ministry.

For example, many congregations form a separate health ministries organization in order to address the wide-ranging health concerns found within any congregation. This health committee sponsors health fairs, organizes education events, and even fosters health screenings. Sometimes these organizations are staffed totally by volunteers. Often, however, the organization supports the ministry of a parish nurse. No matter what the form, a congregation health ministries organization would be well served by joining the Health Ministries Association (*www.hmassoc.org*). HMA is a network for people of faith who promote whole-person health through faith groups in the communities they serve. HMA dues are very affordable and include access to consultation and training, a newsletter, discounts at HMA conferences, and more.

Another national organization that a faith group interested in older adult ministry should consider joining is the National Interfaith Coalition on Aging (NICA) which is a part of the National Council on Aging (*www.ncoa.org*, click on "Constituent Groups" and then click on "NICA"). NICA is seeking to be a leader in providing resources to faith groups in the development of an intentional, focused, and viable older adult ministry. Annual educational/networking gatherings and other resources are available.

NICA joins in participating in an annual educational event with the Forum on Religion and Spirituality in Aging (FoRSA) of the American Society on Aging (*www.asaging.org*, click "About Us" and then "Networks"). A quarterly newsletter of ministry ideas and perspectives, access to names of some of the top thinkers in the area of spirituality and aging, over 20 workshops on spirituality and aging at the annual NCOA-ASA gathering, are but a few of the benefits to joining ASA and FoRSA.

The Christian Association of Senior Adult Ministries (*www.gocasa. org*) is a California based gathering of Christian congregations who are either providing or seeking to provide an older adult ministry within their congregation. Benefits of joining include three quarterly newsletters, one focused on baby boomers, one providing resources for older adults themselves, and a third for leaders. Audiotapes of interviews describing older adult ministry resources and ideas, a member's-only section on the Web site, special tuition discounts to the annual leadership conference, as well as e-mail communications, round out the membership benefit package.

The Center for Spirituality and Ethics in Aging, located in Anaheim, California, has a free, monthly E-mail newsletter designed specifically for faith group leadership and individuals. To subscribe, E-mail: <dkoepke@ frontporch.net>.

An Example of Using Community Organizations in Congregational Ministry

What does a congregational program look like when there is extensive use of community resources? A moderate sized congregation in Orange County, California, has built a significant ministry of support for care-givers within their neighborhood using community resources. By communicating with the local Area Agency on Aging (*www.aoa.dhhs. org*) they collaborated with a county organization called "Caring Connections" and received training and supervisory assistance in developing a "Friendly Visitor Program." This communication and collaboration resulted in a trained group of members who provide weekly friendly visits to older adults in their community who are lonely and isolated, assisting them in securing access to necessary health care and other social service resources.

Second, collaboration with a local caregiving resource center (*www. caregiving.org*) has resulted in a support group for caregivers using facilitators trained and supervised by the resource center. The congregation provides the place for meeting and advertising. The resource center provides the leadership and the program.

The leadership group of the congregation's OAM discovered through a needs-assessment survey that there were two families in the congregation who were struggling with the effects of Alzheimer's Disease. This leadership group connected these families with the local Alzheimer's Association (*www.alz.org*) through which the family not only receives respite services, but education, a support group, and a telephone number to call when the caregiving task becomes too great in the wee hours of the morning.

The congregation is considering joining the Forum on Religion and Spirituality in Aging of the American Society on Aging, and all members who desire receive a free, monthly e-mail newsletter, CSA SPIRIT for CONGREGATIONS *<dkoepke@frontporch.net>*. They also have joined with a cluster of congregations in their area in the sponsoring of an older adult retreat on "The Spiritual Side of Aging." Their congregation had only four members interested in such a retreat, but by joining with other faith groups, the needed number of participants was secured.

So, in the Sunday Bulletin each week, under "Ministries of our Congregation" they list: Friendly Visitors, a support group for caregivers, a ministry with persons with dementia, notification about a monthly newsletter designed for older adults, and an upcoming retreat. The cost to the congregation for all of these ministries: ZERO. The assistance in program and leadership development, and the assistance for their membership: PRICELESS.

Faith Groups Can Offer What Community Organizations Cannot

A faith group can offer older adult services that a community organization cannot. First of all, they can offer insight into the spiritual side of aging. They can "Name the Name" and provide the familiar rituals that touch the soul as well as the body and the mind.

They also have access to the people. The leaders of faith communities can gain access into the homes of persons where community organizations are blocked. Faith groups often have a long-term relationship with people promoting trust and respect. To attend a support group at a home church can feel different from attending the same group at the local senior center.

They have a history of caring for people. It fits the character of a faith group that they provide opportunities for a person to receive the service that is needed at this time in their life. Providing opportunities to be served is an essential expression of faith.

NOTES

1. The motto for the Front Porch Community of Communities, the largest not-for-profit provider of housing for older adults in Southern California is "Doing Good and Doing It Well."

2. When the words Bible Study are entered into Amazon.com, over 16,000 books are found; when the word Prayer is entered over 12,000 books are referenced to choose from to help develop groups and personal growth.

3. E-mail from Christine Driggers to Donald Koepke April 20, 2004 responding to an article "Assessing Spiritual Needs" published in the E-newsletter "CSEA SPIRIT for CONGREGATIONS for March, 2004" by the Center for Spirituality and Ethics in Aging. For a copy, E-mail <dkoepke@frontporch.net>.

REFERENCES

Flemming, A. (1995). Interview with Arthur Flemming as interviewed by James W. Ellor, and Melvin A. Kimble: Center for Aging, Religion, and Spirituality.

Fowler, J. (1995). *Stages of faith: The psychology of human development*. San Francisco: Harper and Row.

Gelfand, D. E. (2003). *Aging and ethnicity: Knowledge and services* (2nd ed.). New York: Springer Publishing Company.

Highfield, M. F., & Cason, C. (1983). Spiritual needs of patients: Are they recognized? *Cancer Nursing, 6*(3). 187-192.

Leder, D. (1997). *Spiritual passages: Embracing life's sacred journey*. New York: Jeremy P. Tarcher/Putnam of Penguin Putnam Inc.

Tobin, S. S., Ellor, J. W., & Anderson-Ray, S. M. (1986). *Enabling the elderly*. Albany: State University of New York Press. 149.

Wili, W. (1954). The history of the spirit in antiquity. In J. Campbell (Ed.), *Spirit and nature: Papers from the eranos yearbooks* (pp. 75-106). Princeton: Princeton University Press.

Worley, R. C. (1978). *Dry bones breath*. Chicago: McCormick Theological Seminary.

SUGGESTED READINGS

Address, R. F., & Person, H. E. (2003). *That you may live long: Caring for our aging parents, caring for ourselves.* New York: UAHC Press.

Bell, S. M. (2000). *Visiting mom: A guide for visiting elders with Alzheimer's.* Sedona: Elder Press.

Bell, V., & Troxel, D. (2002). *The best friends approach to Alzheimer's care.* Baltimore: Health Professions Press.

Byock, I. (1997). *Dying well: The prospect of growth at the end of life.* East Rutherford: Riverhead Books.

Carroll, J. W., & Wade, C. R. (2002). *Bridging divided worlds: Generational cultures in congregations.* Indianapolis: Jossey-Bass Publishers.

Close, H. (2004). *Becoming a forgiving person: A pastoral perspective.* Binghamton: The Haworth Press, Inc.

Eiesland, N. (1994). *The disabled God.* Nashville: Abingdon Press.

Ellor, J., Netting, F. E., & Thibault, J. (1999). *Religious and spiritual aspects of human service practice.* University of South Carolina Press.

Fischer, K. (1998) *Winter grace.* Nashville, TN: Upper Room Press.

Feinstein, D. (1990). *Rituals for living and dying: How we can turn loss and the fear of death into an affirmation of life.* San Francisco: Harper-Collins.

Goldman, C. (2002). *The gifts of caregiving: Stories of hardship, hope, and healing.* Minneapolis: Fairview Press.

Harbaugh, G. L. (1992). *Caring for the caregiver.* Herndon: The Alban Institute.

Johnson, R. P. (1995). *Caring for aging parents.* St. Louis: Concordia Publishing House.

Kahle, P. A., & Robbins, J. M. (2004). *The Power of spirituality in therapy: Integrating spiritual and religious beliefs in mental health practice.* Binghamton: The Haworth Press, Inc.

Kessler, D. (2000). *The needs of the dying: A companion for life's final moments.* New York: Harper-Collins Press.

Kimble, M. et al. (1995) *Aging, spirituality, and religion, a handbook (Vol. 1).* Minneapolis: Fortress Press.

Kimble, M. et al. (2003). *Aging, spirituality, and religion, a handbook (Vol. 2).* Fortress Press.

Lustbader, W. (1991). *Counting on kindness.* New York: The Free Press.

McLeod. (2002). *And thou shalt honor: The caregiver's companion.* Emmaus: Rodale Press.

Moberg, D. O. (2001). *Aging and spirituality: Spiritual dimensions of aging theory, research, practice, and policy.* Binghamton: The Haworth Press, Inc.

Moody, H., & Carroll, D. (1997). *The five stages of the soul.* New York: Anchor Books.

Moore, T. (1992). *Care of the soul.* New York: Harper Collins Books.

O'Brien, M. E. (1999). *Spirituality in nursing: Standing on holy ground.* Boston: Jones and Bartlett Publishers, Inc.

Rando, T. A. (2000). *Clinical dimensions of anticipatory mourning.* Ottawa: Research Press.

Spiro, H., Curnen, M., & Wandel, L. (1996). *Facing death.* New Haven: Yale University.

Tobin, S. S., Ellor, J. W., & Anderson-Ray, S. M. (1986). *Enabling the elderly.* Albany: State University of New York Press.

Topper, C. (2003). *Spirituality in pastoral counseling and the community helping professions.* Binghamton: The Haworth Press, Inc.

Van Hook, M., Hugen, B., & Aguilar, M. (2001). *Spirituality within religious traditions in social work practice.* New York: The Wadsworth Group.

APPENDIX

A Summary of Web Sites

Single Disease Organizations (research, support, education)

The Alzheimer's Association *www.alz.org*

American Heart Association *www.americanheart.org*

American Stroke Association *www.strokeassociation.org*

American Diabetes Association *www.diabetes.org*

National Multiple Sclerosis Society *www.nmss.org*

ALS Association *www.alsa.org*

National Parkinson Association *www.parkinson.org*

National Council on Aging *www.ncoa.org*

National Interfaith Coalition on Aging *www.ncoa.org*

Benefits Check Up *www.benefitscheckup.org*

Benefits Check Up for Medications *www.benefitscheckuprx.org*

Agency on Aging *www.aoa.dhhs.gov*

National Alliance for Caregiving *www.caregiving.org*

National Academy of Elder Law Attorneys *www.naela.org*

National Site: Agency on Aging *www.aoa.dhhs.gov*

Ombudsman, Local Services, Medicare Questions

American Association of Homes and Services for the Aging *www. aahsa.org*

Not-for-Profit Long-Term Care–Communities and Services

National Association of Professional Care Managers *www. caremanagers.org*

National Association of Home Care *www.nahc.org*

Health Ministries Association *www.hmassoc.org*

American Society on Aging *www.asaging.org*

Forum on Religion, Spirituality and Aging (FoRSA) *www. asaging.org*

Christian Association of Senior Adult Ministries *www.gocasa.org*

CSA SPIRIT for CONGREGATIONS E-mail: *dkoepke@ front porch.net* (A free monthly E-mail newsletter)

Spiritual Need Five:
Providing Quality Pastoral Care
as a Congregation

Robert A. Rost, DMin

SUMMARY. Critical to the needs of older adults is the care and nurturing of the feelings and emotions that often offer context for the human spirit. Grounded in the history of pastoral care, this chapter explores an approach to pastoral care that is reflective of the author's study and experience in the parish. *[Article copies available for a fee from The Haworth Document Delivery Service: 1-800-HAWORTH. E-mail address: <docdelivery@ haworthpress.com> Website: <http://www.HaworthPress.com> © 2005 by The Haworth Press, Inc. All rights reserved.]*

KEYWORDS. Meaning, spiritual, caregiving, pastoral care, holiness, communal dimension, ministry

INTRODUCTION

This chapter will be more reflective of a Christian perspective only because of the limitations of my own personal experience and professional competence. Still, I do hope that it will further inter-faith dia-

[Haworth co-indexing entry note]: "Spiritual Need Five: Providing Quality Pastoral Care as a Congregation." Rost, Robert A. Co-published simultaneously in *Journal of Religion, Spirituality & Aging* (The Haworth Pastoral Press, an imprint of The Haworth Press, Inc.) Vol. 17, No. 3/4, 2005, pp. 121-153; and: *Ministering to Older Adults: The Building Blocks* (ed: Donald R. Koepke) The Haworth Pastoral Press, an imprint of The Haworth Press, Inc., 2005, pp. 121-153. Single or multiple copies of this article are available for a fee from The Haworth Document Delivery Service [1-800-HAWORTH, 9:00 a.m. - 5:00 p.m. (EST). E-mail address: docdelivery@haworthpress.com].

logue among other religious perspectives about the spiritual dimension of our common humanity and how this needs appropriate attention and care.

Faith communities themselves extend to the whole global range of religious traditions as well as encompassing a variety of contexts from a continuum of care facility to a neighborhood congregation. While my own thirty years of ministry is parish-based in the Roman Catholic tradition, I have come to appreciate that faith communities can take many forms wherever and however God's people gather and relate to one another in God's name and God's love.

The term *pastoral care* most often refers to a compassionate outreach toward those experiencing pain or woundedness, whether the primary expression of that pain or woundedness is physical, mental, emotional, interpersonal, or spiritual. Some find the term "pastoral" too defined by denominational membership, official religious ritual, and the ministry of the ordained "pastor." Some would much prefer the term "spiritual" care as a way of avoiding such limitations and labels. While I concur that such ministry should not be limited in these ways and certainly not labeled as valid or invalid by these expressions, I employ the term pastoral care because of the historical and theological roots of this ministry.

Pastoral care as a term is generally differentiated from the term *pastoral counseling*. While pastoral care is the more general term, pastoral counseling denotes a specific relationship between a counselor and a counselee. Thus this term is employed in pastoral counseling centers and in other specific contexts where intentional counseling takes place. Pastoral care often includes some elements of pastoral counseling in the broader sense that any helping relationship employs some counseling techniques and short term, often crisis oriented counseling interventions. However, for the parish pastor and lay leadership, to offer ongoing counseling presents potential role conflicts in the life of the parishioner and time and resource constraints for the pastor.

HISTORICAL AND THEOLOGICAL ROOTS

From this perspective, the ministry of pastoral care is grounded in the fundamental mission of the faith community, which in the classic tradition of Christianity is called the *cura animarum*, or the care of souls. This tradition dates back at least to the sixth century (Oden, 1984, Chapter 2). The first major articulation of the extent of this responsibility (*cura animarum*), particularly for pastors (bishops and priests) was the

Regula Pastoralis by Gregory the Great, who served as Pope from 590-604. In this work he advises pastors on how they ought to counsel the many kinds of persons for whom they bear pastoral responsibility.

> Long before my time Gregory Nazianzen, whose memory we hold in honor, taught that no single exhortation suits everyone because we are not all bound by the same character traits. What helps some often harms others. Teachers have to accommodate their language to the characters of those who are listening to them so as to meet their individual needs, but they must never renounce the art of building up everyone. The art of preaching demands great diversity. (Oden, 1984)

His fundamental principle in this work is *juxta uniuscuiusque qualitatem*, i.e., "in accordance with each one's character." That is, the care of the soul is not "one size fits all" but rather unique to the individual character of this particular soul. He comments at varying length on thirty-six pairs of qualities or character traits (Leinenweber, 1998, x-xi). Gregory's enumeration of qualities for the care of souls ranges from circumstances of birth to characteristics of personality, qualities of motivation, life choices, and life situations beyond individual choice. The pastor's duty is to attempt to discern the unique opportunities and dangers of a whole range of characteristics and circumstances, most of which are far beyond the personal experience of the pastor, which makes this principle quite a challenge to practice.

Gregory's thirty-six pairs are actually the pairing of polar opposites. Using this method he demonstrates, by the radical comparison of one extreme to another, that no matter what character trait dominates one's life situation or personality, each person has both a unique grace and a unique temptation in relation to his or her call to holiness. No person is without the unique grace or the unique temptation as created in the *imago Dei* (the image of God) and with a human nature that is prone to stray away from God.

Some persons' temptations may seem more obvious because their character traits can tend toward more obvious or public failings. Other persons' temptations are much more subtle because their character traits can appear to be ready-made for sanctity. Gregory indicates that this latter category of people actually needs greater care of their souls so that the more subtle temptations do not go undetected and thus become as deadly as the more obvious ones. No one is ready-made for salvation or damnation. Each soul, no matter what the dominant character trait, has the capacity for grace and sin. Each soul needs care, by the person and the pastor, for sanctification to be assured.

Thus, key to Gregory's model of the care of the soul is the discernment of the specific grace and temptation unique to each and every person as well as to his or her relationships and responsibilities. Given the fact that he developed this approach over a millennium before the birth of modern philosophy and psychology, his insights into the human person are quite phenomenal. His model is also quite free of the platonic dualism (body vs. soul) the Church inherited from Augustine, which makes it quite useful as a foundation for a wholistic approach to pastoral care.

While he distinguishes persons by personality, relationships, and responsibilities, he isn't interested psychosocial symptoms and treatments but rather the care of the soul which is the core image of God within the person. The ultimate purpose of soul care is the whole journey of the soul toward sanctification and salvation. Since his model of pastoral care is not crisis intervention, psychological counsel, or social work, its unique focus, in an interdisciplinary setting, would distinguish it from these other disciplines. This would also help clarify the role of the pastoral caregiver in such settings where that clarity has been absent far too often.

The trust factor would be absolutely critical to the practice of spiritual discernment in Gregory's mode. A person does not just "bare one's soul" to just anybody at any time. A person would need both reason and opportunity to make such intimate disclosures. The pastoral caregiver would have to prove worthy of such trust not only in terms of confidentiality but even more so in terms of the spiritual wisdom to assist the person in processing the realities of grace and temptation as they emerge in his or her life. I am humbly reminded of this every time I enter into a pastoral conversation. "Lord, help me to prove worthy of this person's trust."

BIBLICAL ROOTS

For those of us who approach pastoral care from the Judeo-Christian tradition, we seek to ground our ministry not only in our historical roots but also in our Scriptures. John Patton asserts that the most fundamental Biblical basis for pastoral care resides in "the Old Testament faith in the memory of God and the New Testament conviction that Jesus as the Christ is evidence of God's remembering" (Patton, 1993, 29). "In the

Old Testament there can be no dichotomy between God's thought and action, that God's remembering always implies God's movement toward the object of God's memory" (Patton, 1993, 28-29). The memory of God is "virtually equivalent to his acts of deliverance" (Patton, 1993, 29). This belief and the corresponding call upon the memory of God's people are foundational to Biblical spirituality. The words "remember" and "remembered" occur 280 times in the Scriptures. These passages are all testimonies to the memory of God's saving love and to the primary response of God's people to remember and not forget who they are and whose they are. The paradigm Patton proposes would view "pastoral care as a ministry of the Christian community that takes place through remembering God's action for us, remembering who we are as God's own people, and hearing and remembering those to whom we minister" (Patton, 1993, 15).

Remembering God's action for us, remembering who we are as God's people, and hearing and remembering each other are all essential to the exercise of the mission of the *cura animarum* throughout its whole range of pastoral expressions from sacraments, to catechesis, to evangelization, to peace and justice initiatives. The care of souls exists in but is not limited to the one-on-one encounter. It can and should permeate all ministries as well as the very character and mission of the community toward and beyond its own membership.

The communal dimension of this Biblical spirituality is paramount in two ways. First, in this paradigm, pastoral care becomes a ministry of the congregation, by the congregation, for the congregation. It is not just the possession of the pastor(s). It is a fundamental expression of the priesthood of all believers. While this seems so basic and obvious, it demands a fundamental paradigm shift for most congregations and institutions of care. In many of them, pastoral care still resides only in the hands of the ordained and/or certified who, in their job description, are not required to bring others of the community into this ministry. These others would include the natural caregivers of the person or family as well as professional and para-professional caregivers. Until this fundamental shift takes place in the pastoral leadership, the communal dimension of this spirituality will not be recognized or nurtured. Programs such as Stephen's Ministry and BeFriender Ministry, which offer models of training and supervision for lay pastoral caregivers, are very appropriate expressions of putting this paradigm into practice.[1]

Second, "remembered means to re-member. It means to put the body back together. The opposite of remember is not to forget, but to dismember" (Patton, 1993, 28). This communal dimension of re-membering ministry is even more critical in the pastoral care expression of the *cura animarum* because the experience of woundedness, whatever the source or symptom, can and does tend to dismember persons from community, and community from those persons. It requires conscious, intentional effort on the part of the community, whether family or congregation, to overcome the physical and spiritual forces of dismemberment. The experience of woundedness is a true wilderness journey where belonging must be demonstrated by presence and not taken for granted in absence.

Note that the mission of *cura animarum* also has a dimension of individual responsibility. Each person has a responsibility and a capacity to care for his or her own soul, not outside community but within community. When persons are wounded they may well need our pastoral care to assist them, but they are still responsible for and capable of their own soul care. Ninety-nine percent of soul care takes place outside the pastoral encounter where the person and/or family are on their own. What they do for themselves and each other is the most critical part. Thus, the focus of the pastoral encounter should be on not only the dynamic of the present interaction but also the influence of the past, as well as the responsibility for the future. The encounter needs to be empowering for the person, not just a comfort.

SACRED REMEMBRANCE IN SOUL CARE

Sacred remembrance, i.e., the searching of one's memories for the presence and purpose of God, is an essential part of that soul care. When we engage in pastoral care ministry, it is essential that our ministry affirm and empower that person's responsibility and capacity for this kind of remembrance. Through active listening and responsive prayer we assist persons in remembering God's action for them, remembering who they are as God's own children, and hearing and remembering the voices of their own souls. It is the voices of our own souls that we hear in our sacred remembrance. Our members need to become as attuned to the voices of their own souls as they are to the voices of our sermons.

Those of us who preach need to be mindful of our responsibility to empower people in this regard. As Gregory says, "the art of preaching demands great diversity" (Leinenweber, 1998). Pastors could even utilize brief sacred remembrance exercises in their sermons to assist their congregation in actively practicing soul awareness at the heart of the liturgy. Have the congregation close their eyes and stay awake. Take them to their storehouse of memory and select one that exemplifies the current focus of the Word. Let this memory have their entire attention so that the presence and message of God contained therein may become clear to each one. Their receptivity to the power of Word and Sacrament will be greatly enhanced by the liturgical practice of listening to the voices of their own souls.

I have found this to be a very good practice in my preaching. It is an act of pastoral care to each and every person in the assembly who chooses to participate. By having them connect their own very personal memories with the message of the Word, the Word becomes personally incarnate and the spiritual meaning of the memory comes to light. Thus, the Word becomes memorable and the memory becomes a revelation.

The memory of God and the deliverance of God is mediated through very human experiences, relationships, and interactions. For people of faith, both in Biblical times and in our current era, there is no such thing as personal stories which say nothing about God. This may seem like a rather bold claim to make. Yet, is it that our stories are impoverished of the presence of God, or, rather, that our stories tend to be more emotive descriptions of experience rather than spiritually interpretative of said experience? What does my own story say to me? For example, is my coronary procedure just the experience of the latest medical technology or a wake-up call to mortality and the gift of divine patience with my conversion?

James Empereur would claim "that it is impossible to speak about God without also speaking about oneself " (Empereur, 1987, 91). It is our story that holds our past, present and future together in a meaningful way. The current search for meaning through the occurrences and encounters of our own reminiscence becomes a sacred search as much as the Hebrews in search for the promised land or the disciples bereaved journey to Emmaus. Particularly for those facing serious losses or painful transitions, the darkest of valleys, the search involves critical questions about God's deliverance as well as feelings of being left out or left behind by the main-stream of life that most us take for granted.

The Bible not only provides spiritual and theological legitimacy for engaging in sacred remembrance; it also demonstrates how much divine presence and purpose can be revealed in very human stories of all kinds. The Scriptures become both a role model and a motivator for us to remember, share and interpret our own and each other's stories. And, conversely, the more we are in touch with our own stories and their meanings, the more alive and powerful the stories, images and metaphors of the Scriptures become. The process of reminiscence would be greatly impoverished in the absence of the Scriptures and, likewise, the study of the Bible impoverished in the absence of the process of reminiscence. Both need each other for the meanings of our lives and the Reign of God in our midst to be revealed, celebrated, and chosen.

When I went on my first Sister Parish delegation to El Salvador in the midst of their civil war, I was so terrified while I was there I could barely pray much less reflect. Yet as soon as I returned to my parish and read the Scriptures I had to preach on that following Sunday, the intensity of my experience released the power of the Word which, in turn, interpreted my reality. I was the man born blind in John chapter nine, and I had never realized that until I left the insulation of my own country to set foot in the world of my sisters and brothers.

Our stories contain the sacred memories which tell us who God is for us and who we are for God and with one another. It is the vocation of each and every person of faith to recall and to interpret his or her own sacred memories. It belongs to the part of soul care for which I, and I alone, am individually responsible. No one can do this for me nor can anyone prevent me from exercising this responsibility. Yet, like every other part of my vocation from God, I need help and encouragement. In the exercise of individual, spiritual responsibility "inter-dependence, not independence, is the true gospel value" (Church, 1999, 3). The Scriptures attest to this responsibility in the harvest ritual of Deuteronomy 26, the Emmaus story of Luke 24, and Jesus' image of the learned scribe in Matthew 13. The Bible gives us life reviews of Moses (Deuteronomy 32 & 33), Jeremiah (Jer 15:10-21; 20:7-18) and Paul (2 Corinthians 11:16-12:10; Phil 3:2-11) as testimonies of God's call turning their lives around for the deliverance of God's people.

It is the mission of each and every community of faith to provide opportunities for these stories to be shared and celebrated. Early in my ministry, an African-American woman asked me where, in the Catholic Church, was there room for testimony. Both her question and my lack of an answer were very telling for how we were/are neglecting this fundamental part of our mission. We hold members responsible for their own soul care but we do not provide adequate opportunities and encouragement for this to be developed and practiced. We certainly have plenty of room for the catechesis of the community on church doctrine but have to ask for permission to inspire the community by testimony. Paul says in 1 Corinthians 12:7, "To each person the manifestation of the Spirit is given for the common good." The manifestation of the Spirit in our sacred memories is not just for private edification but for mutual inspiration. For more than one denomination and congregation there still needs to be a paradigm shift in their pastoral practices to make "plenty good room" in pastoral encounters, faith-sharing groups and congregational assemblies for the personal manifestations of the Spirit to be heard and received.

As the process of reminiscence is impoverished by the absence of the Scriptures, so the local faith community is impoverished by the silence of the sacred memories of its members. Unfortunately, such impoverishment too often goes unrecognized in those communities who have yet to begin to make such "plenty good room." If you have never seen it, if you have never experienced it first-hand, if your faith has never been fulfilled or challenged by the integral and interdependent connection between your Scriptures and your sacred memories, then you have not begun to realize how impoverished you are. Likewise, as this connection takes intentional shape in sermons, in sacraments, in catechesis, in group process, in pastoral care encounters, then and only then will the manifestations of the Holy Spirit be recognized and nurtured throughout our communities in their narrative structure.

From a gerontological point of view, this would apply very specifically to the memories of its elder members. Harry Moody asserts that there is critical connection between the life reviews of older adults and the common good. He holds that there is a "loss of faith in the continuity of a public world, a world beyond the self" (Moody, 1984, 159). The life review of older adults, which tells the story of the human journey from birth until death, which reveals the sacredness of all life, is essential to the recovery of the public world. He sees it as "the best guidance, perhaps the only guidance, that one generation can give another" (Moody, 1984, 158).

According to Charles Gerkin the sharing of sacred remembrance would not only be critical to the recovery of the public world but would be vital to the discovery of an eschatological identity in which the pilgrimage of the self "is joined with that larger pilgrimage of all persons, all aspects of existence" (Moody, 1984, 159). My story is not just my story. My story being heard by another is not just my feeling that I am not alone. The Scriptures tell me that my story is part of a much larger, longer, historical, eschatological, universal Story. I am part of a people who are all on the same pilgrimage toward communion with God and, in God, with each other.

Mel Kimble asserts that older adults become our teachers through their own experience of aging (Kimble, 199, 124-125). They are witnesses who are qualified to give living testimony to the lifelong journey of faith. Peter, identifying himself as a "fellow elder" in 1 Peter 5:1, appealed to them to shepherd the flock by their example. In John 21:18,

Jesus prophesied how Peter himself, in his old age, would give his most powerful testimony of faith and courage to the community.

A short while back, our family entered into a caregiving journey with our parents which concluded in both of them going home to God over the course of six months. During this time, I found out that they, once again, would be for us, their children and grandchildren, our teachers. While we were trying our utmost not to be overwhelmed by the challenges of their caregiving, they were teaching us how to face the process of dying with faith and courage.

For the elderly to become our teachers, for the younger generations to come to believe that longevity holds great meaning and divine purpose, the stories of our elders, sensitively heard and spiritually interpreted, need to be heard within our faith communities. Often times this level of sensitivity is heightened in the process of caregiving for those who are dying or grieving for those who have completed the journey. Oftentimes it is only then that the stories reach their true significance in the souls of those who hear and tell them. This has been my consistent experience in congregational pastoral care with caregivers and those who are grieving, as well as in our own family experience and stories throughout our parents' home going. Again, these are all prime times for testimony which has great spiritual significance to both family and community.

James Birren and Donna Deutchman attest that "from the viewpoint of human development, there is little of greater importance to each of us than gaining a perspective on our own life story, to find, clarify, and deepen meaning in the accumulated experience of a lifetime" (Birren & Deutchman, 1991, 1). They make a strong case for this practice of life review and for engaging in this practice in a group setting, especially if the group is inter-generational.

Their work teaches us to encourage and empower people to tell and listen to their own story, their own meanings and interpretations, and to do that within an interpersonal context. Here we can see sound psychology reinforcing and validating sound spirituality. We can also begin to notice the sheer wealth of opportunities we have within the local faith community to engage in this encouraging and empowering work.

Another resource for the local congregation would be the work of Richard Morgan (Morgan, 1996). His workbook is explicitly rooted in Biblical imagery focusing the reminiscence on how my story intersects with the Story of salvation. His exercises on God images, family relationships, mid-life crises, healing of memories, and preparation for eternity are very fruitful in heightening the soul's awareness of its own journey of conversion. Still, his most fruitful contribution is awakening in us the awareness of the unfathomable wealth of enlightenment for our sacred remembrance we have in the Scriptures. After doing every exercise in his workbook one realizes that one has only begun to mine the mother lode of meaning contained in our Scriptures.

Some congregations utilize a Lectionary-based Scripture reflection methodology to develop faith-sharing groups. When such reflection and sharing is brought together with spiritual journaling, there can be ample opportunity for sacred remembrance to occur in a prayerful and communal setting.[2]

After having practiced these combined disciplines together over the course of eight Lenten observances, I can testify to the abundance of soul care that is nurtured in this manner. The journaling empowers people to relate to the Scriptures in far more personal ways than they ever thought possible. The Scriptures encourage and challenge the journaling to take on a more soulful depth and intimacy with God. The journal-sharing that happens in small, confidential groups validates the individual soul care and enables spiritual bonding to take relationships to greater depth and solidarity. The intergenerational setting helps the participants to listen to the other voices and to liberate their minds from cultural stereotypes which impede real relationship.

Such approaches as these would not only serve the ministry of adult education but that of pastoral care. Their primary goal is not new information but rather longitudinal formation. As we engage with our own life experience, with the Scriptures God provides, and with persons from our own faith community, we are being formed in that eschatological identity which places us squarely in the larger and longer pilgrimage toward the Kingdom.

SPIRITUAL NEEDS ARISING
FROM CHRONIC PHYSICAL CONDITIONS

Still, such group opportunities, while they nurture and challenge many persons of every generation, are not inclusive of every older person. In any local faith community setting, two primary contexts of pastoral care with older adults are experiences of chronic physical conditions and other life transitions evoking fundamental changes in attitude and meaning.

Those who suffer from chronic physical conditions and advanced age are in danger of losing touch with their own capacity to find meaning in their lives, past as well as present. In light of this harsh reality, Harold

Koenig articulates twenty-five spiritual needs of physically ill elders. They are as follows:

Needs related to self

1. A need for meaning and purpose
2. A need for a sense of usefulness
3. A need for vision
4. A need for hope
5. A need for supporting coping with loss and change
6. A need to adapt to increasing dependency
7. A need to transcend difficult circumstances
8. A need for personal dignity
9. A need to express feelings
10. A need to be thankful
11. A need for continuity with the past
12. A need to accept and prepare for death and dying

Needs related to God

13. A need to be certain that God exists
14. A need to believe that God is on our side
15. A need to experience God's presence
16. A need to experience God's unconditional love
17. A need to pray alone, with others, and for others
18. A need to read and be inspired by scripture
19. A need to worship God, individually and corporately
20. A need to love and serve God

Needs related to others

21. A need for fellowship with others
22. A need to love and serve others
23. A need to confess and be forgiven
24. A need to forgive others
25. A need to cope with the death of loved ones (Koenig, 2004).

Obviously, these needs are present in every person, of every age and of every health condition. Any of us can both relate to all of these as well as get in touch with how they are each a part of our spiritual pilgrimage at every stage of the journey.

But, for older people who suffer from chronic physical conditions, such basic human needs may well become more acute and it can no longer be taken for granted that they are being met as a matter of course. These conditions may compel persons to confront existential issues that they previously could avoid or deny. They may also give rise to questions of identity and self-worth. When I asked a room full of professional pastoral caregivers to comment on Koenig's list of needs, they saw both personal and spiritual significance to every need he articulated.

In my mind, from the very limited experience of caregiving with our mother until her passing and finding so many similarities with the experiences of other family caregivers, the condition of dementia may well have its own sub-set of spiritual needs for both the person as well as the family.

For one's self, there is the need to accept and even transcend the progressive loss of short-term memory and other cognitive abilities as well as all the reliance we place on that for our identity and purpose in life. Thus, there is the need to live both in the limitations of the moment as it happens as well as in the long-term memory for as long as it can be accessed. One's personal dignity lies in who he/she has been their whole life as well as who they are just being from moment to moment.

For one's relationship with God, there is the need to experience and believe in God's unconditional love in spite of the condition of the dementia. As Paul writes in Romans 8:39, "Nothing can separate us from the love of God that comes to us in Christ Jesus." There is the need to experience this in worship, individually and communally, in ways that do not depend on short-term memory. The prayers, the songs, the rituals, the Scriptures and the symbols, which were memorized earlier in life and are indelibly marked on the soul so deep that nothing can take them away, become *the* most significant pathways to God.

They also become the equalizer between those who suffer from dementia and those who do not. Both can equally give and receive in the same communal worship experience. As Paul writes,

> None of us lives as his own master and none of us dies as his own master. While we live we are responsible to the Lord, and when we die we die as his servants. Both in life and in death we are the Lord's. This is why Christ died and came to life again, that he might be Lord of both the dead and the living. But you, how can you sit in judgment on your brother? Or you, how can you look down on your brother? We shall all have to appear before the judgment seat of God. It is writ-

ten, 'As surely as I live, says the Lord, every knee shall bend before me and every tongue shall give praise to God.' (Rom 14:7-11, NAB)

For one's relationship with others, there needs to be those who know and love them for who they have always been as well as those who understand and accept them for who they are now under these circumstances.[3] Both of these groups of persons, oftentimes the family caregivers and the trained professionals respectively, need to partner with each other in sustaining the person's dignity, security, and care. Both of these groups need to help each other find the ways that continue to connect them with the person in spite of the progressive and irreversible nature of the disease.

If the person has the long-term past experience of religious tradition, the interpersonal connections multiply by continually tapping into that wellspring. Even after the debilitations of progressive dementia and a major stroke, on her eighty-third birthday, our mother could still make the sign of the Cross, recite all the responses of the Catholic Mass, sing hymns by heart, join in the Lord's Prayer, and receive Communion as she always had since she was seven. We were never more connected with our mother than when we were all engaged in prayer together. The very prayers that she taught us as children we could still pray with her under these circumstances which were such a cross both to her and to us. These, indeed, became not only our spiritual comfort food but our very manna as we wandered in the wilderness.

Here in this realm of those older adults who suffer from chronic and progressive physical conditions, including dementia, we find the true risk and challenge of the aging process and the real questions for gerontological pastoral care:

- What kind of listening, interpreting and empowering does it take on the part of the caregiver, pastoral or personal, to affirm these persons' dignity, to make the meanings of their past more accessible, and the possibilities of their present and future more clearly grasped?
- How much does that caregiver need to be able to care for the whole person, both the one who was before as well as the one who is now?
- Within the faith community, what kind of support for and listening to caregivers and their stories is most respectful and empowering for their relationships?

I hope to address these as we continue this exploration.

SPIRITUAL NEEDS ARISING FROM CHANGE IN MEANING AND ATTITUDE OF OLDER ADULTS

The second gerontological context giving rise to special spiritual needs, the process of older adults undergoing a fundamental change in meaning and attitude, has been studied by Richard M. Erikson (1995). The key elements he highlights as integral to this process are: *biographical reconstruction* and *indispensable plausibility structure.*

Biographical reconstruction refers not to any attempt to alter the facts of history, but rather to alter one's *interpretation* of the facts of history. We remember not just the bare facts, but our emotions and our interpretations of them. When one is undergoing a major transition of whatever kind, one is changing the interpretation and meaning of one's life, of one's history, thereby maintaining a sense of continuity and coherence about one's life.

When our dad was diagnosed with pancreatic cancer, his fundamental task in life changed from being primary caregiver to his wife of sixty-one years to being a person, under palliative care, facing his final journey home. For the final three months and five days of his life, his relationship with God, his relationship with each member of his family, and his relationship with his own soul shifted to face the unknown challenges of this journey.

Indispensable plausibility structure refers to any and every way that this transition process and, thus, this process of biographical reconstruction is being supported by significant others who share the same set of meanings and attitudes. The biographical reconstruction, integral to the transition process, needs the indispensable plausibility structure to maintain itself in an ongoing fashion.

The fundamental shift in our dad's health status required a corresponding shift in all of us who became his and mom's caregivers. It required all of us to break through our denial and avoidance in order to relate to them appropriately as well as to take up all the responsibilities of the caregiving and the homegoing. In short, they had to become more dependent on us and we had to become more dependable in order for them to stay in their own home throughout his final journey. In this case and most assuredly in others, it seems that the biographical reconstruction was actually mutual rather than one-sided and the indispensable plausibility structure was the fundamental shift in our whole family system rather than a one-way giving to our parents.

These elements of biographical reconstruction and an indispensable plausibility structure are critical to the process of facing life-transitions, chosen or unchosen, which require persons to redefine their identity and relationships. Older adults facing chronic physical conditions, as well as those who would naturally accompany them, enter into such a process. When assisting them, it is vital for the pastoral caregiver to realize that this is a fundamental shift in role and relationship for everyone. Thus, the pastoral caregiver needs to operate not in a vacuum but rather in collaboration with the natural caregivers, medical professionals, social workers, support structures such as Hospice and the Alzheimers Association. All of these are part of the extended indispensable plausibility structure that helps the older adult and his/her primary caregivers make these difficult transitions.

The pastoral caregiver needs to also be aware of the boundaries and limitations of his/her role in order to be most respectful and helpful for the older person and the natural caregivers. In the course of our caregiving with our parents, I had the gift of observing the professionals who were the most respectful and helpful. These are they who always knew their place in the process, who respected the voice and choice of the elder, who supported responsible family deliberations, decisions, and actions, who, while letting the elder and his/her family into their heart, always remembered whose journey this was and whose it was not.

If sacred remembrance is an integral part of facing the transitions of one's life, including those which involved chronic, progressive physical conditions in the context of fundamental shifts in personal identity and primary relationships, then such remembrance is not just about the past but is also about the future. It involves not only remembering but anticipating.

When I spent ten days in the hospital last fall recuperating from the unanticipated complications from what was supposed to be a simple in-and-out surgery, I spent hours each day walking the halls of the fifth floor with my IV tree contemplating my mortality for the first time in my life. The significance of my brush with possibly becoming a fatality or permanently disabled propelled me to finally anticipate the inevitable outcome of my life on this earth and the meaning that holds for me and my life choices now.

GERONTOLOGICAL PASTORAL CARE
AND THE REALM OF MEANING

The question, then, is not only what meanings does one find in one's past but also what meanings does one anticipate and strive toward in one's future. The realm of meaning has been most thoroughly explored by Viktor Frankl and given gerontological application by Melvin Kimble. Both would say that focused reminiscence serves to strengthen and complete our very integrity of life.

Frankl asserts that it is not that we are asking the question "what is the meaning of life?" but rather that we are the ones being asked by life. "In a word, each man is questioned by life; and he can only answer to life by answering for his own life; to life he can only respond by being responsible" (Frankl, 1984, 113). He claims that the transitoriness of life adds to our responsibleness. And "in the past, nothing is irrecoverably lost but everything is irrevocably preserved and saved, safely delivered, and deposited." Once we have realized a value or fulfilled a meaning, we have "fulfilled it once and forever." Nothing can take that away from us. Memory is the means by which we access these meanings and values from the "full granaries of the past" (Frankl, 1988, 74).

Melvin Kimble would say that we should never underestimate the importance of remembering. "Memory enables us to hold fast to our identity and to shape and interpret it in new ways. We do not merely have these memories; we are these memories" (Kimble, 2000, 124). In them we find our coherent sense of self and the foundation for our ongoing integrity of life. Meaning is discovered in the interpretations we give to the experiences we have already had and to the current opportunities life presents to us.

In our pastoral care with older people, we need to listen for the interpretations they give to their own experiences as well as assist them in searching for these meanings. Thus, we enable them to "become our teachers through their own experience of aging" (Kimble, 2000, 115). This is why Kimble would refer to "life review as a method of mutual ministry" (Kimble, 2000, 124). It is a ministry of interpreting and sharing as well as listening and learning.

Our parents taught us more about facing the realities of aging and dying in the last months of their lives just by being themselves in the midst of their journey home than I had learned in all my ministries and studies. They were not only our first teachers of life; they were our last teachers of life as well. The teaching and the learning were in the relationships, which is a vital revelation in itself.

Frankl perceives this search for meaning as taking shape in three distinct groups of values. "The first is what he gives to the world in terms of his creations; the second is what he takes from the world in terms of encounters and experiences; and the third is the stand he takes to his predicament in case he must face a fate which he cannot change" (Frankl,

1988, 70). Ethically speaking, Frankl asserts that we are responsible for what we create, whom we love, and how we suffer (Frankl, 1988, 124). I find this perspective is very helpful precisely because it emphasizes personal and interpersonal responsibility and opportunity in a comprehensive way that is applicable to all elders in any and all circumstances. We are both capable and responsible for finding meaning in what we create, whom we love, and how we suffer for as long as we live.

As we are already learning with our more positive attitudes toward aging, later life can be a very creative time for many elders. It can hold many opportunities for loving relationships, old and new, peer and intergenerational, to blossom and thrive. Learning how to lovingly grasp another person in his or her innermost core only increases with age and experience. These are the more obvious opportunities for those who are engaged in them. Yet, in our pastoral care, we should not take them for granted, because both the opportunities and the motivation for these may need some encouragement and assistance. Finding meaning in an older person's life does not just happen when they are in prayer with us. As I alluded to earlier, ninety-nine percent of their meaning-making needs to happen beyond the pastoral encounter.

Interestingly enough, about ninety-nine percent of the time and energy I spent with our parents in their journey home and with our family was not in the professional role of priest or pastoral caregiver but appropriately shifting my practical functioning and interpersonal relating as son, brother, and uncle.

Frankl's second group of values refers to human relationships. He holds that each person establishes unity and completeness with a community, not within him or her self (Kimble, unknown). In love, human beings have the capacity to transcend themselves to grasp another in his or her innermost core, which holds not only the person's character but also his or her potential. "Furthermore, by his love, the loving person enables the beloved person to actualize these potentialities. By making him aware of what he can be and of what he should become, he makes these potentialities come true" (Frankl, 1984, 116).

Frankl's description of the power and capacity of love is akin to the Scripture's revelations about the love God has for us, e.g., in Jeremiah 31:31-34, Ezekiel 36:24-28, John 15:9-17, Philippians 1:6 and 1 John 4:7-16. Thus, according to the Scriptures, this kind of love has a divine origin which takes on incarnate human form when a person's heart is purified and empowered by the love of God. Because of this kind of love's capacity to grasp the potential of the other person, it is most often associated with the love of the parent for the child or of the lover for the beloved. Yet this is the same kind of love that JoAnn Kimble, Mel Kimble's wife, described as essential for the adult child in becoming the primary caregiver for his or her own parent. She described it as a love one had to grow into as the relationship had to radically change over the course of the caregiving and the homegoing.

Reflecting on our family's experience of caregiving with our own parents, I would whole-heartedly agree. It is only because our parents had this kind of love for us as children growing into adults that we could grow into having something of that love for them through their final journey home. Since it is divine in origin, this kind of love in families may be an incarnation of the spiritual law attributed to Jesus him-self–"the measure you measure with will be measured back to you" (Luke 6:38, NAB).

SUFFERING AND THE SEARCH FOR MEANING

Because of our natural and logical avoidance of suffering, the most difficult learning curve in our responsible search for meaning in life is in *how* we suffer. Frankl holds that "attitudinal values are the highest pos-sible values," the *how*, and that "the meaning of suffering–unavoidable and inescapable suffering alone, of course–is the deepest possible meaning" (Frankl, 1988, 75). For, if there is meaning in the attitude one takes toward unavoidable suffering, then "life's meaning is an uncondi-tional one" (Frankl, 1984, 118). Neither suffering nor dying can detract from it. Thus, "life never ceases to hold a meaning, for even a person who is deprived of both creative and experiential values is still chal-lenged by a meaning to fulfill, that is, by the meaning inherent in an up-right way of suffering" (Frankl, 1988, 118). But the ultimate meaning of human suffering cannot be grasped by the human intellect because it ex-ists in a higher dimension than thought. What people need is "uncondi-tional faith in unconditional meaning" (Frankl, 1988, 156). And it is Frankl's contention "that faith in the ultimate meaning is preceded by trust in an ultimate being, by trust in God" (Frankl, 1988, 145).

Prior to our caregiving with our parents, I already shared Frankl's conviction about the ultimate meaning of human suffering based on nu-merous sources including Scriptural revelation, testimonies of saints and mystics, pastoral care encounters, and my own limited life experi-ences processed in prayer, and spiritual direction. Through the course of our family's experience of our parents' home going, my conviction of deepened enormously. This happened in the course of watching my parents each progressively give up everything they possessed externally in their lives and internally within their own bodies while maintaining unconditional faith throughout their suffering grounded in unshakable trust in the God who never abandoned them. This was their choice. The same choice they had been making their whole lives with whatever suffering they faced. But, for as strong as their will power was, they were the first to confess that the real power to face suffering came from God. "In the One who is the source of my strength, I have strength for everything" (Phil 4:13, NAB).

Thus, in the realm of suffering and attitudinal values, the ability to behold grace is indeed a grace, the grace of faith preceded by the grace of trust.

> Now that we have been justified by faith, we are at peace with God through our Lord Jesus Christ. Through him we have gained access by faith to the grace in which we now stand, and we boast of our hope for the glory of God. But not only that–we even boast of our afflictions! We know that affliction makes for endurance, and endurance for tested virtue, and tested virtue for hope. And this hope will not leave us disappointed, because the love of God has been poured out in our hearts through the Holy Spirit who has been given to us. (Romans 5:1-5, NAB)

From his fullness we have all received, grace upon grace (John 1:16, NRSV).

Frankl and the Scriptures are, indeed, correct. Maintaining a meaningful attitude in the midst of suffering is not a matter of the intellect but rather grace upon grace which is sought out, prayed for and chosen.

The Scriptures, especially, focus our attention on the revelation of what grace *we* have received. It is in this realm of grace in the face of suffering that both individuals and community are challenged to affirm their interdependency as members of the same Body of Christ sharing the same Spirit (Catholic Church, 1999, 3).

Whatever form the suffering takes, physical or mental, interpersonal or spiritual, or any combination thereof, the homeostasis of both the person and the Body is disrupted and anxiety is created. With this disruption and concurrent anxiety come a whole host of temptations: scapegoating, victim thinking, binding anxiety through triangling, avoidance, denial, rescuing, patronizing, distancing, etc.

While I had observed this phenomenon countless times over the course of thirty years of pastoral care, six months of family caregiving taught me how powerful this disruption and concurrent anxiety can be. Even in "functional" families with every external resource and support necessary for the entire journey, there is the whole host of temptations in every member and throughout every relationship. I very quickly became aware that this journey was going to bring out all our "warts and demons." Not only once but twice during our caregiving journey, I initiated and presided over the sacrament of reconciliation with general absolution with our family. I did this not to magically wipe away all the temptations or sins, but to reinforce our need for divine mercy and deliverance. Because the caregiving journey takes such a toll on the soul of each and every member involved, we must turn to God as *the* source of our strength.

These temptations become the attitudinal focal point. They highlight the choice of attitude which suffering places before each person involved. What attitude will I choose to take toward my own suffering? What attitude will I choose to take toward the suffering of someone I dearly love? What attitude will I choose to take toward both the suffering and the attitude of the person suffering with whom I am called to extend pastoral care?

The choices of attitude made by each one of us in our family came forth from our history of attitudinal choices toward suffering. Only now these were highlighted by the unique experiences of both our parents' journey home as well as our heightened interdependence in caregiving. Thus, for better and for worse, we saw sides of ourselves and of each other that we had not seen that clearly before.

Obviously, there are interrelational implications to these choices of attitude.

> Death is the single most important event in family life. From an individual point of view it marks the end; from a family point of view it is often a beginning that initiates processes in the family that can continue for generations. More cut-offs begin and more reconciliations are accomplished during this passage. More shifts in responsibility occur. It is more likely that some family members will find new freedom, and some will suddenly find themselves stuck. During the death rite of passage, secrets allow the demons an opening into the next generation. (Friedman, 1985, 168-169, 172)

Spiritually, the choices of attitude determine whether the relationships are conducive or not conducive of grace specifically in the face of suffering.

These interrelational implications for each one of us in our family came out of our history of relationships toward each other, only now intensified by the interdependence and intimacy of the caregiving. Where relationships were basically healthy, they became more so. Where they were already conflicted, they became more so. Where personal responsibility resided, it increased. Where victim thinking resided, it increased as well. Both internally and interpersonally each of us was changed by the process. These interrelational implications did not stop with the end of our parents' suffering and their going home. A year later, for better and for worse, they are very much present and influencing the shape of our family ties.

These choices of attitude, which suffering demands, cannot just be made once-for-all, but must be continually reviewed and renewed as long as the suffering lasts. Thus, it is, indeed, "grace upon grace" which must be sought out, prayed for and chosen.

Again and again, our choice of attitude had to be reviewed and renewed once our dad went home and our mom was left behind. Executing the decision to place our mom in a special care unit was more difficult than letting our dad go. Just because the decision is right, doesn't make it any less difficult nor the appropriate attitude any more automatic. Most fortunate for us, our mom was still very capable of traditional prayer and we were able to place her in a Catholic nursing home run by Franciscan sisters who knew her for a long time. Often and together we prayed for the right attitude, for her suffering did not cease until she rejoined her husband.

These choices highlight how much suffering is *the* test of our trust. Suffering tests not only our trust in the God who will ultimately bring victory over suffering (Revelations 21:1-11), but also our trust that each and every one of us is given a manifestation of the Spirit for the common good here and now (1 Corinthians 12:7). In the courageous choices of attitude, which transcend the temptations generated by the suffering, the Spirit is manifest and the victory has begun.

In our family's journey, this truth was more readily seen is the attitudes of our parents than in our own. Whether that was because it was their journey home and not ours or whether they were just more courageous about it than we were, I do not know. But their attitudes were certainly a much needed and appreciated inspiration for our own choices. Once again, they were not only our first teachers in the ways of faith, but our last teachers as well.

Charles Gerkin asserts that the grace of such trust is grounded in the Gospel's fundamental revelation. "Suffering thus replaces power and omnipotence as the primary characteristic of God." In the event of the Cross, both Father and Son suffer in the act of abandonment. Now, for all time, Jesus "is to be sought wherever there is human suffering." He identifies with all who suffer and long for redemption. The Holy Spirit "is to be found wherever there is suffering in the not-yet-ness of the final unity of all things." The Spirit works in history as the "creator of a new future" (Gerkin, 1984, 67).

Faith in these Biblical truths is essential for Christian caregiving, whether pastoral, clinical, or personal. This faith forms the spiritual bond with the person which strengthens the attitude toward suffering of all involved. Fortunately, for our family, dad and mom led the way in that faith.

The capacity to transcend the attitudinal temptations human suffering generates takes the grace of the Spirit as creator of a new future. This is where Frankl's three categories of values merge together. The development of the attitudinal value of finding meaning and beholding grace in the midst of suffering requires creative and loving work which is both ours and God's. When the old attitudes will no longer work, the new attitudes must be created. When the actual has reached its limits, the potential must be grasped, and can only be grasped in love–love from God, love from another, and love from one's own self.

When our family sat down with the hospice personnel at the beginning of our parents' journey home, they described in very practical terms the journey ahead of us as a family. From the standpoint of the medical and the practical, their description was very accurate. While they touched on the attitudinal and the interrelational dimensions of the caregiving, I do not think we were ready to fully hear that part. Only when our old attitudes no longer worked and our actual relationships reached their limits were we face-to-face with the challenge of creating the new and realizing the untapped. This was, in fact, far more difficult than the practical.

Frankl describes a practitioner of his school of logotherapy as more of an ophthalmologist than a painter, i.e., not conveying to the client a picture of the world as he or she sees it but rather "widening and broadening the visual field of the patient so that the whole spectrum of potential meaning becomes conscious and visible to him" (Frankl, 1984, 114-115).

In his dying process, our dad did not need his son-the-priest nor any chaplain to paint him a pretty picture of heaven. But he did appreciate his son, his daughter, and his hospice nurse listening to the meaning of his dying as the letting go of his place in assuring for mom's care, especially as her needs accelerated with the advance of her dementia. Logotherapy, like the discernment of Gregory's model of pastoral care, encourages and empowers the person to find his or her own meaning in the cross that is uniquely theirs.

PASTORAL CARE AS THE ART OF INTERPRETATION

This combined approach of Frankl and Kimble in the search for meaning raises a critical question for the pastoral caregiver. What awareness is necessary to develop this interpretive ability, particularly with persons facing significant losses and transitions in their lives, and specifically from the perspective of faith? Charles Gerkin addresses this question (Gerkin, 1984).

He perceives that "all understanding of human experience is fundamentally historical: meaning and meaningfulness are contextual" (Gerkin, 1984, 42). The path to understanding of a person's experience is through his or her own personal story. The person is, literally, a living, human document. When the interpretation of the personal story becomes blocked, when the connection between experience and idea becomes too painful, the person must search "for a listener who is an expert at interpretation, one who can make sense out of what has threatened to become senseless" (Gerkin, 1984, 26).

Yet such an expert needs to have gone through his or her own process of "pre-understanding," which Gerkin calls a "hermeneutical detour," in order to enter into another's language world without doing violence. He would see this process of self-awareness as "a continuous process of question and correction, refinement, and integration." Such a process would reveal, not only one's biases, but also one's limits and capacities for assisting in the interpretation of this particular person's story and accompanying language world. It would also be essential in order that "both interpreter and the object of interpretation are to be changed at the fundamental level of meaning" (Gerkin, 1984, 44-46, 57, 61).

Herein lies one of Gerkin's most valuable insights into the art of pastoral care. Growth in the art is not just how many pastoral care courses or seminars or units of CPE one has accumulated. It is not just in one's professional certification, religious ordination or graduate degrees. It is not just in one's ability to quote the most popular works in the field. Growth in the art is in direct proportion to one's growth in self-awareness which is a continuous and never ending process of being challenged by the responsibilities and relationships of one's life as well as learning to listen to the voice of one's own soul.

While I have been blessed with some wonderful academic mentors who have led me in processing the revelations of my professional ministry, even more critical to my growth in self-awareness has been my work in spiritual direction and in therapy. It is here that I processed the revelations of my life, my family, my close relationships and the grace and sin of my own spiritual journey. It is here that I confronted my fears and discouragements, my trust and boundary issues, my prejudices, my cultural and religious biases, my victim thinking, and my dependencies.

While this interactive process of living and reflecting is definitely hermeneutical in that it is ongoing interpretation and re-interpretation of my life, I never saw the process as a "detour" but rather as the inward and outward journeys necessary for the healing and health of both soul and psyche. As Birren attests, "from the viewpoint of human development, there is little of greater importance to each of us than gaining a perspective on our own life story, to find, clarify, and deepen meaning in the accumulated experience of a lifetime" (Birren & Deutchman, 1991, 1).

While I did not intentionally enter into this ongoing, interactive, hermeneutical process of living and reflecting for the purpose of advancing the art of my pastoral care, over time I can discern a direct co-relation between the growth of the former and the advancement of the latter. The most personal and humbling learning of my own self-awareness has been the most critical to my appreciating and assisting in the learning curve of other pilgrims on the journey. Likewise, the challenges of my accompanying those who carry the heaviest of crosses make me even more aware of not letting my issues and biases get in the way of their finding healing and redemption. In all, I find this co-relation to be a hermeneutic circle of growth that is a most sacred trust and one that constantly brings us back to "the Source of all our strength" (Philipians 4:13).

Gerkin's envisions the life of the soul as one of continuous interpretation, i.e., a life of attaching meanings to behavior, relationships and one's ongoing identity. At the center of this structure of meaning lie the questions of faith and ultimate purpose. God is the "power that participates in all the force/meaning influences upon the life of the soul." Using this image of the person's ongoing process of interpretation, sacred remembrance would be the level of the process which seeks center of meaning where one can most clearly detect the power of God (Gerkin,

1984, 102-105). Again, this brings us back to the historical and theological roots of pastoral care in the *cura animarum*.

Like Birren, Frankl, and Kimble, Gerkin perceives the road to authenticity as "the road to integration of mutually dissociated aspects of the self." The task of interpretation is seen as that of removing certain blockages to integration and an opening of the way toward greater wholeness. Gerkin's view of wholism is not only that of overcoming the fragmentation of the self but that of approaching the wholism of an ecology of relationships. From a Christian eschatological point of view, the hope for an ecology of transformed relationships lies in the transformation of all things in Christ. "The work of creative transformation involves both suffering and waiting for the work of the Spirit" (Gerkin, 1984, 146-156).

I do have much more appreciation for Gerkin's notion of a "wholism of an ecology of relationships" since our caregiving journey as a family. That names what we were striving for, for our parents' sake as well as our own. While we fell short of the goal, we made great strides while being stretched by the challenge. I would also say that the "wholism of overcoming the fragmentation of the self " may well be an essential ingredient to the larger wholism. At least for me, the work of overcoming my own fragmentations I was able to do on a prior sabbatical enabled me to enter into our family process with much greater capacity and willingness. I believe that the two are interdependent. For me, the internal was foundational for the interpersonal.

So "the counseling relationship is itself seen as subject to the power of the Spirit at work in the mediation between history and eschatology," i.e., between the interpretation of past, present and future in light of the ultimate meaning which only God can provide. And this relationship is set within a very specific ecology of relationships of authentic Christian community. "Only a community of shared vision and narrative structure can meaningfully sustain the level of continuing dialogue and shared experience that makes the continuation of a Christian life of pilgrimage possible" (Gerkin, 1984, 71, 179).

Going back to the beginning of this chapter, the primary mission of the local faith community is the *cura animarum*, the care of souls. The more one has realized this "very specific ecology of relationships of authentic Christian community," the more this mission is able to be fulfilled. Conversely, the less one has this type of communal relationships the less this mission is able to be fulfilled. Over time, consistently solid pastoral care ministry builds up community and can be found in all truly community building activities. More recently I have discovered that even in fund raising for our new church and in disciplining children in our school there is pastoral care, because the real issues are not just money or behaviors but persons and relationships. Seen in this light, responsibility for the building up of an authentic spiritual community has far more ownership and leadership than a single ministry, but rather it reaches into all ministries (Friedman, 1985, 210-212).

Sacred Resources for the Art

I have found that it is within this context of pastoral care in the hermeneutical mode that the most appropriate use of both Scripture and prayer (including ritual and sacramental prayer) come to light. Such usage requires knowledge, freedom and presence, i.e., knowledge about the integrity of these sacred resources, the freedom to use them as instruments of the Spirit, and being as completely present to both the person and the Spirit in a prayerful encounter as one can be at that moment. One's knowledge and freedom as minister increases in direct proportion to one's being present to both persons and the Spirit in these sacred encounters. In Gerkin's language, the person as a living, human document and the Spirit as the creator of a new future are the most challenging and motivating of teachers. Every pastoral caregiver should enter each and every pastoral encounter aware of the need to be taught by both the person and the Spirit.

One of the surprising ways my own knowledge, freedom and presence increased dramatically over the course of our family caregiving was in the use of the traditional Catholic practice of praying the Rosary. While my own preferred spirituality of pastoral practice tends to gravitate toward a combination of the Scriptural, the sacramental, the spontaneous, and the testimonial, *the* prayer form our entire family can engage in fully and equally is the Rosary on our knees, the same way our parents taught us to pray when we were children. It was amazing to see how less anxious and more centered we all became upon praying this way together. Subsequent to this revelation with my own family, I began to try it with other families who had similar devotional backgrounds in my pastoral practice, to much the same result. Thus, the question–what is more important, the preferred spirituality of the pastoral caregiver or the most familiar spiritual food of those being cared for? The answer, in each situation, needs the guidance of the Spirit.

John Patton offers some guidance and some admonition on how one's personal stories should be related to the Biblical Story. He would hold that specific human experiences "do not demand a particular theological conclusion." Rather, they can be "most effectively interpreted with a soft focus of symbolic and sometimes multiple meanings." By "soft focus" he would refer to the process by which the pastoral caregiver assists the person in developing a clearer focus on the meaning emerging from within his or her experience. He would conclude that "the witness of faith in the midst of life is mostly metaphor" (Patton, 1981, 157-168).

As the pastoral caregiver develops the art of hermeneutical focus, a "hard" dogmatic focus actually becomes more foreign to the encounter and the story, while a "soft" parabolic focus actually becomes more natural and effective as it changes both persons at the fundamental level of meaning. The term "focus of illumination" may more accurately describe the purpose and outcome of the process of bringing one's personal story into communion with the Biblical story, in much the same way as Jesus did with the two disciples on the road to Emmaus (Lk, 24:13-35). He actually had them take a "hard" look at their own Scriptures to come to a burning recognition of His identity and mission. I believe that the use of Scripture in pastoral care is always about illumining the darkness which accompanies suffering.

Elaine Ramshaw (1987) states that the minister "needs to provide a range of images, Biblical stories, and other rich symbols in prayer that emphasize the connection between ritual and the human need for meaning." "When prayer grows out of listening, it can be a way into the need, rather than a way around it." Thus, as the person's stories are shared and brought to prayer, it becomes clear that "all the person's experience is worthy of God's own attention." This can be done in prayers of praise as well as petition, and even lament. Indeed, the pastoral caregiver needs a whole range of spiritual resources to respond to persons' needs for prayerful accompaniment.

Essential in striving for that goal is to remember to be more of an eye specialist than a painter in responding to the person's stories. "One day Jesus was praying in a certain place. When he had finished, one of his disciples asked him, 'Lord, teach us to pray'" (Lk, 11:1). This is literally what our listening to a person in the pastoral care encounter should do, i.e., teach us how to pray, and conversely not to pray, with them.

When my sister and I discovered that our dad was holding back his own dying process, not because of any fear of death, but out of concern for what would happen to our mom, then, and only then, did we know how to appropriately respond to him in conversation and in prayer.

Within those religious traditions which are more Eucharistic, when the pastoral care visit involves celebrating the Eucharist with those who cannot come to Sunday Liturgy, the encounter can become an even more appropriate occasion for such sharing and listening. For the Eucharist is the Memorial Meal through which we remember, make present, and anticipate *the* saving action of God in the death, resurrection and future coming of Jesus Christ. Following the command of Jesus, "Do this in remembrance of me," the Meal makes the Story come alive. There is no better time for our sacred stories to be shared and celebrated, to witness to the greatness of our God. There is no better way for us to make the connection between our memories and the Memorial of our very salvation. There is no better moment for our sense of time, as embedded as it is in our own history, to be transformed by this eschatological encounter with the risen Christ.

This, of course, requires the minister of the Eucharist to enter into the person's story prior to and during the ritual, "when prayer grows out of listening." If the minister's attention is on only the ritual, he or she will miss the person and the story. If the minister prays only the words prescribed in the ritual book, then the prayer never grows out of but rather is disconnected from the listening. Again, the primary mission of the encounter is the *cura animarum* of the persons entering into the Eucharistic encounter rather than merely following the rubrics meant to serve said sacred encounter.

As Empereur would say, the human need for meaning, in particular, is intimately connected with the Eucharist as "the central continuing enactment" of our identity as a priestly and a pilgrim people. For the physically ill older person, "the Eucharist can be a powerful sign of the bond of community within the Body of Christ which transcends all isolation." Thus, in the sharing of the elder's sacred memories during the Eucharistic encounter, the elder not only remembers and is remembered but also is re-membered in the community to which they give priceless testimony of the unfailing and saving memory of God (Empereur, 1987, 60-96).

At our parish we have developed a ritual of sending forth Eucharistic ministers to the sick as part of our Communion Rite in the Mass. We do this with the following prayer. "All good and gracious God, our sisters and brothers who are sick, who are homebound, who are caregivers are always in your redeeming hands. May our prayers and our affections accompany them, today and every day, so that we may become ever mindful of their cross and of their witness. We ask this through Christ our Lord. Amen." On both sides of the relationship, the Eucharist is meant to keep us re-membered.

Yet as powerful and as foundational as the Eucharist is to the living of our baptismal life in many faith communities, it is not the only ritual which certain Christian traditions offer to sustain us on the journey. The Lutheran, Anglican and Roman traditions each offer extraordinarily similar rituals which bring together confession and anointing with the Eucharist (Pfatteicher, 1983, chapters 3 & 5). This "ritual of rituals" was designed specifically for those who are undergoing serious illness, the disabilities of advanced age or the dying process itself. Whether celebrated together or separately, confession and anointing provide unique opportunities for sacred remembrance to be lifted up in prayer.

The sacred remembrance is twofold in each ritual. In confession, we are called to remember the saving mercy of our God at the same time as we remember our need for that mercy because of the sins. In anointing, we are called to remember the healing touch of Jesus which set people free at the same time as we remember our need for that healing because of the difficulties which beset our body and soul.

In each ritual, we are called to a conversion experience, i.e., to remember our sin and/or our sickness not just as a manifestation of human frailty but as an occasion of divine power and redemption. Such conversion does not happen magically but rather through an intentional and ongoing hermeneutic encounter through which blockages to change are interpreted and thus lifted. When united with the Eucharist, these two rituals bring forth the full meaning of the Sacred Meal. Eucharist is our communion with the One who forgives us our sins and who offers us salvation for our bodies and souls, now and forever.

As I stated earlier, I presided over two reconciliation services with our family during our caregiving. The first was in the context of this "ritual of rituals" involving the Mass. While not having any perceived magical or miraculous results, we all felt called to a conversion experience to see, with eyes of faith and trust, this journey not only as the occasion of suffering, temptation, and sin but also of divine mercy, redemption, and remembering. Most of us had a good cry as well, which reinforced our vulnerability to the presence of the One who was calling us.

FINAL EXHORTATION

The full power of ritual, sacred remembrance and pastoral care is released only when there is close connection and collaboration between the community's pastoral caregivers and natural caregivers. "Emotional process in religious organizations not only mirrors emotional process in personal families, but also, both types of family systems plug into one another. The deepest effects that both systems have on one another come from the fact that they both run on the same current, if not the identical energy source. The influence is internal rather than external. They are plugged into one another and their respective states of homeostasis join in a new overall balance" (Friedman, 1985, 195, 198).

I confess I did not realize the full import of this fundamental revelation until our family became the natural caregivers. While I never really got out of the role of "the-son-the-priest or the-brother-the-priest," the first-hand experience of family caregiving taught me more about "emotional process in personal families" than any other experience I have had in my own family or with the families in my congregations over thirty years of ministry. In our churches we focus a lot of energy on collaboration among professional caregivers, and rightly so, because for too long pastoral care was the domain of only the ordained. But our collaboration needs to be stretched much further to be as inclusive of the natural caregivers as possible for we are indeed all plugged into "the identical energy source," "the Source of all our strength" (Phil 4:13), the One who "is love" (1 Jn 4:8).

Often times this is not possible because of a number of practical obstacles to being together at the same time and place as well as some spiritual hurdles due to unresolved religious conflicts. When it becomes possible, both the pastoral and the family systems become plugged into the same spiritual current that energizes everyone, especially the person who is the focus of everyone's care. Ritual and ministry take on their most natural form in which each and every person involved is "a manifestation of the Spirit given for the common good" (1 Cor 12:7, NAB).

From all that has been said thus far about the integral nature of sacred remembrance to congregational pastoral care, it would seem essential that pastoral caregivers would be in the process of their own sacred remembrance. This could be Gerkin's hermeneutic detour or, in my terms, the inward and outward journeys necessary for the healing and health of both soul and psyche.

Writing one's own spiritual autobiography, spiritual journaling, entering a faith-sharing or 12-step group, being a member of a "base Christian community," taking the journey of therapy and/or spiritual direction would be some of the options open to ministers to facilitate this process. The processes of ministry and faith reflection which are integral to chaplaincy training as well as Befriender Ministry certainly encourage growing self-awareness as well as further reflection beyond the group sessions.

Beyond those settings of formal training, the utilization of the processes outlined in Mahan, Troxell, and Allen's *Shared Wisdom: A Guide to Case Study Reflection in Ministry* and Killen and DeBeer's *The Art of Theological Reflection* in a ministry support group could be extremely helpful to one's pastoral care. While those of us with CPE training under our belt may cringe at the thought of voluntarily doing a "verbatim" and submitting it to group critique, I have found that these processes of case study and theological reflection can be a very positive experience of genuine reflection for anyone's ministry. Most of us take far too few opportunities for such reflection, which can be a disservice both to us and to those for whom we care.

If there is anything that my thirty years of pastoral ministry along with my continuous and unending hermeneutical journeys have taught me, it is this. The initiatives we take to courageously explore our own story in all its humanity are absolutely essential to any and all ability we have to encourage and empower others to interpret theirs. The ongoing care of our own soul is essential to our making any positive and graced contribution to the *cura animarum.* "If I speak with human tongues and angelic as well, but do not have love, I am a noisy gong, a clanging cymbal" (1 Cor 13:1, NAB). The elders of our faith communities require and deserve more than noisy gongs and clanging cymbals.

NOTES

1. Stephens Ministry, 2045 Innerbelt Business Center Drive, St. Louis, MO 63114-5765 (314) 428-2600. BeFriender Ministry, University of St. Thomas, St. Paul Seminary, 2260 Summit Avenue, St. Paul, MN 55105-1094 (651) 962-5775.

2. This method of sacred remembrance has been developed and utilized since 1997 by Dr. Robert Rost, Nativity of Mary Church, 10017 East 36th Terr, Independence, MO, 64052.

3. From a conversation with JoAnn Kimble, social worker and primary caregiver for her mother, during the winter before her mother's going back to God.

REFERENCES

Birren, J. E., & Deutchman, D. E. (1991). *Guiding autobiography groups for older adults.* Baltimore: Johns Hopkins University Press.

Catholic Church (1999). *Blessings of age: A Pastoral message on growing older within the faith community: A statement of the U.S. Catholic Bishops.* Washington, DC: United States Catholic Conference.

Empereur, J. (1987). *Worship: Exploring the sacred.* Washington, DC: Pastoral Press.

Erikson, R. M. (1995). *Late have I loved thee.* New York: Paulist Press.

Frankl, V. (1984). *Man's search for meaning.* New York: Simon and Shuster.

Frankl, V. (1988). *The will to meaning.* New York: Penguin Books.

Friedman, H. (1985). *Generation to generation.* New York: The Gilford Press.

Gerkin, C. (1984). *The living human document.* Nashville: Abingdon Press.

Kimble, M. A. (1990). Aging and the search for meaning. In J. J. Seeber (Ed.), *Spiritual maturity in the later years.* Binghamton: The Haworth Press, Inc.

Kimble, M. A. (2000). *Viktor Frankl's contribution to spirituality and aging.* Binghamton: The Haworth Press, Inc.

Kimble, M. A. (unknown). Frankl's ten theses on the human person. *Center for Aging, Religion, and Spirituality.*

Koenig, H. G., & Lewis, G. (2004). *The healing connection: The story of a physician's search for the link between faith and health.* West Conshohocken: Templeton Foundation Press.

Leinenweber, J. (Ed.). (1998). *Gregory the Great, Pope, Pastoral Practice: Books 3 and 4 of the Regula Pastoralis.* Harrisburg: Trinity Press.

Moody, H. (1984). Reminiscence and the recovery of the public world. In M. Kaminsky (Ed.), *The uses of reminiscence.* New York: The Haworth Press, Inc.

Morgan, R. L. (1996). *Remembering your story: A guide to spiritual autobiography.* Nashville: Upper Room Press.

Oden, T. C. (1984). *Care of souls in the classic tradition.* Minneapolis: Fortress Press.

Patton, J. (1993). *Pastoral care in context: An introduction to pastoral care.* Louisville: Westminster/John Knox Press.

Patton, J. (1981). Clinical hermeneutics: Soft focus in pastoral counseling and theology. *The Journal of Pastoral Care, 35*(3), 157-168.

Pfatteicher, P. (1983). *Commentary on the occasional services.* Minneapolis: Fortress Press.

Ramshaw, E. (1987). *Ritual and pastoral care.* Minneapolis: Fortress Press.

Spiritual Need Six:
Community Building

Judy Armstrong Bever, MDiv

SUMMARY. Community building includes but is greater than providing fellowship. Community building promotes connection, belonging, and a sense of togetherness. Based upon the needs of older adults, community building is defined as an engagement that is mutually supportive and stimulating. Community building doesn't just happen naturally. There are important guidelines and categorization that assist in effective planning. Community building can happen any time a person is personally engaged with another and thus, with some intentionality, can happen at worship, committee meetings, as well as pot lucks and fun activities. *[Article copies available for a fee from The Haworth Document Delivery Service: 1-800-HAWORTH. E-mail address: <docdelivery@haworthpress.com> Website: <http://www.HaworthPress.com> © 2005 by The Haworth Press, Inc. All rights reserved.]*

KEYWORDS. Community, connection, belonging, spirituality, guidelines, basic, intermediate, growing deeper

---

[Haworth co-indexing entry note]: "Spiritual Need Six: Community Building." Bever, Judy Armstrong. Co-published simultaneously in *Journal of Religion, Spirituality & Aging* (The Haworth Pastoral Press, an imprint of The Haworth Press, Inc.) Vol. 17, No. 3/4, 2005, pp. 155-167; and: *Ministering to Older Adults: The Building Blocks* (ed: Donald R. Koepke) The Haworth Pastoral Press, an imprint of The Haworth Press, Inc., 2005, pp. 155-167. Single or multiple copies of this article are available for a fee from The Haworth Document Delivery Service [1-800-HAWORTH, 9:00 a.m. - 5:00 p.m. (EST). E-mail address: docdelivery@haworthpress.com].

155

WHY IS COMMUNITY BUILDING IMPORTANT IN OUR CHURCH?

Albert McClellan, in an article directed toward his pastor, attempted to explain what seniors need. The need to belong ranked number two on his list:

> The aged want to be accepted and to belong . . .
> There are exceptions, but most want to be heard by others with hearing that pays attention, and they want to belong to the group with the belonging that is accorded equality. (McClellan, 1989, 23)

One of the first formal theories to try to explain the aging process was the "disengagement theory." Developed by Elaine Cumming and William Henry in 1961, the theory said in part:

> In our theory, aging is an inevitable mutual withdrawal or disengagement, resulting in decreased interaction between the aging person and others in the social system he belongs to. (114)

Many other observers of the aging process disagreed with this disengagement theory. They found that seniors often wanted to be engaged with their society and that it was society which pushed the seniors into isolation by excluding them and demeaning their efforts. Thus, the opposite end of the social involvement continuum came to be expressed by the "activity theory" by Bernice Neugarten and Robert Havighurst:

> Whereas the disengagement theory emphasizes withdrawal from roles, the activity theory stresses a continuation of role performances. In this view, when roles are lost, such as in retirement and widowhood, the individual is expected to find substitutes. . . . The activity theory holds that society withdraws from the aging person, but this is against the person's will or desire. To minimize this withdrawal, the person must try to be active, keep busy, and stay "young." (Harris, 1990, 114)

Neither of these theories adequately explained what happens to people as they age and many other theories were formulated in an attempt to do that very thing (Moberg, 2001). Rather than focus on one issue to describe what seniors need, perhaps it is more useful for the purposes of ministry with older adults to look at a broad range of senior needs. Many lists of such needs exist. One of the most helpful has been formulated by David O. Moberg. He suggests the following overlapping categories:

- *The Need for Meaning and Purpose* . . . The need for meaning and purpose relates closely to the deeply ingrained desire to maintain one's personal dignity and self-esteem.
- *The Need for Love and Relatedness* . . . Sharing companionship, conversation, intimacy, laughter, a hug, or caressing touch and giving oneself to others by work or service help to satisfy this need.
- *The Need for Forgiveness* . . . Most of us have experienced failures . . . these can be resolved through accepting the forgiveness of God and of others.
- *The Need for Spiritual Integration* . . . We need to know and to feel ourselves spiritually integrated beyond our own existence into an absolute order of existence.
- *The Need to Cope with Losses* . . . even losses can enrich one's life journey for each provides an opportunity for spiritual growth and development.
- *The Need for Freedom to Raise Questions* . . . usually, it is cathartic for people to share . . . questions with a sympathetic listener.
- *The Need for Flexibility* . . . old age is a period of life in which many changes are imposed upon people, despite whether they desire and seek them.
- *The Need to Prepare for Dying and Death* . . . much of this preparation seems purely physical and materialistic . . . but also old emotional accounts from past mistakes and grudges can be settled.
- *The Need to Be Useful* . . . This is a form of the need to love others and in turn, to receive love from others.
- *The Need to Be Thankful* . . . The life review can stimulate a more balanced perspective that includes one's happy experiences, profitable accomplishments, and good circumstances (Moberg, 2001, 162-166).

While it may be possible for an older adult to meet these needs in isolation, for most seniors these needs are better met through engagement with another. For example, there are some seniors who prefer to cope with their losses in private. However, for many others the support of others as well as a safe place to tell their story and have their emotions validated is essential. Evidence of this is the plethora of self-help groups to deal with loss. There are divorce recovery groups, groups for widows, groups for

parents of murdered children, groups for people dealing with various physical losses, and the list goes on.

The same could be said for every need on Dr. Moberg's list. It might be
possible to meet these needs in private, but they may be better met in community. All of which brings us back to the truth of Mr. McClellan's statement about the need for seniors to be accepted and to belong. Belonging is
more than simply being active–more than keeping busy. Belonging has to
do with being engaged with others in meaningful ways. Belonging means
more than just knowing someone's name. Belonging means being in a relationship with others that allows time for nurturing, support, and fun!

Recent research has shown that this need for belonging is so strong that
it may even affect one's health and longevity. According to Macarthur
Foundation Study of Aging in America (which was begun in 1987), one of
the key factors in predicting strong mental function in old age is "a strong
social support system" (Row & Kahn, 1998, 19).

It is not only mental functions which are enhanced by engaging with
others, but also physical health is improved:

> It turns out that active mental stimulation, and keeping up relation-
> ships with friends and relatives, also help promote physical ability.
> For instance, many people are surprised to learn that frequent emo-
> tional support (listening, encouragement, cheering up, understanding
> and so one) is associated with improved function in old age. . . . A
> healthy physical and emotional lifestyle seems to be of greater value
> to older people than to younger ones. (Row & Kahn, 1998, 27-28)

Besides mental and physical functioning, there is one more aspect of a
senior that is enhanced by engaging with others. That is spirituality. In
1975, The National Interfaith Coalition on Aging defined spirituality in
this way:

> Spiritual well-being is the affirmation of life in relationship with
> God, self, community, and environment that nurtures and celebrates
> wholeness.

Notice the emphasis on "in relationship." While reflection and meditation may enhance one's spirituality, one needs to be engaged with others
for that spirituality to grow and deepen. Ben Johnson said it even more
forcefully:

Spirituality from the Christian perspective must include a relation with fellow believers in the Christian community. (Johnson, 1989, 126)

All evidence points to the undeniable fact that seniors need to belong. Being engaged as a part of a community has a positive impact on all aspects of life–mental, emotional, physical, and spiritual. Yet becoming engaged with others doesn't just happen. It takes time and place and intention.

There is one institution that is uniquely structured to provide these elements and to help seniors build a sense of belonging and that is the church. Building belonging and community uses what a congregation does naturally–gather together.

WHAT IS COMMUNITY BUILDING?

Simply stated, community building is a process that allows people to engage with one another. The common introductory act of sharing one's name is community building. If you add to that some other piece of sharing such as where one was born, you have moved a little deeper into community because people now know something else about each other and are beginning to discover similarities as well as differences. Again with time, effort and intention, this process can move to the point where individuals are comfortable sharing from the depth of their souls.

Because community building involves self-disclosure, some guidelines are necessary to enable community building to lead toward positive outcomes of participants feeling comfortable, having fun, and becoming more engaged with each other.

Guidelines for Community Building

1. *Community Building happens best in a supportive atmosphere:* First of all, it is imperative for the leader to have a positive, confident, fun attitude. A leader who can model the sharing and laugh at his/her own foibles does much toward establishing the atmosphere for others. A comfortable environment is also important. Will the group be okay standing for this exercise or would chairs be helpful? Is everyone going to be able to hear? Is the temperature okay?

2. *Everyone is in charge of his/her own sharing:* No one should ever be forced to share something they do not want to. "I pass" is always an accepted, respected answer. Further, no one should share for someone else without permission. "Bob had the neatest definition of God. Is it okay if I share that, Bob?" It is not the purpose of community building exercises to pull out deep, dark secrets. It is the purpose of community building exercises to open doors to sharing–but it is up to the individual to decide when she/he is ready and willing to go through them.

3. *Everyone has a chance to talk and be heard by someone:* There's one in every crowd–you know the one that wants to dominate the conversation. It is important that each person have a chance to be heard. For this reason, community building exercises are often done in groups of two or three. Even in smaller groups, it is helpful for the leader to "mark time" by reminding everyone when it is time for someone else to talk.

4. *Community Building Exercises need to be appropriate for the group mix:* Is this a gathering with people who don't know each other very well (or at all)? Or is this the Sunday school class that has been meeting every Sunday for the past thirty-five years with the same members attending? Or is it a mixed group of new members, long-time members, and guests? If there are folks new to the group, be sure to use community building exercises that will help them feel welcome and included (see some of the suggestions under "Basic Ideas").

5. *Community Building Exercises need to be appropriate for the setting:* A church pot luck dinner celebrating birthdays is probably not the best place to ask people to share their deepest grief! When planning community building exercises, keep in mind the purpose of the event. Is it a celebration and do you want to have fun? Is it a Bible Study class and members want to know each other better? Is it Sunday worship and time is limited?

6. *As Groups move deeper in their sharing, confidentiality is essential:* Anything that anyone shares of a personal nature needs to be treated with respect. As members of groups grow in their trust of one another, they will begin to share important and sometimes painful issues and struggles. It is imperative that confidentiality be the rule and that it be stated often, at least at the beginning and at the ending of each group meeting. "What is said in this group stays in this group."

7. *Everyone's story is unique and important:* Sometimes people begin to judge their own story in light of the others that they have heard. "O, I was just a housewife. I never went to college or did anything important like you." Where would we be without those wonderful, nurturing housewives! Each person's story/life is important and it is essential that none be dismissed as inconsequential. No one's story is better, more spiritual, more triumphant, etc., than anyone else's. We are all made in the image of God!

HOW IS COMMUNITY BUILDING DONE?

Community building exercises come in all shapes and sizes and levels of intensity. For ease in our purpose here, we will look at them in three general categories: Basic, Intermediate, and Going Deeper.

Basic

These are great for groups who do not know each other or for welcoming newcomers into an existing group. Basic exercises allow people to get to know a little more about each other beyond their name. They are frequently called "get acquainted exercises" or "icebreakers." They require very little risking on the part of the participants.

Examples

Introductions: for groups up to 25 (otherwise it takes too long):

1. Give each participant a piece of paper and ask them to write down their name, their favorite color, the last good movie they saw, their favorite TV show.
2. Divide the group in pairs and have them share their lists.
3. Now, have the pairs introduce each other to the larger group.

Ha: for 8-20 people[1]:

1. Have people sit or stand in a circle.
2. First person says "Ha"; Second person says "Ha-Ha"; Third says "Ha-Ha-Ha." You get the idea.

3. See how many you can get before folks break out in laughter. You can either go all the way up as many as there are people or it's over when people laugh.

Analogies: for any size group (for large group, form smaller groups of 5-6):

1. Go around the group sharing analogies such as: "If I were a car, I would be . . ." or "If I were an animal, I would be . . ." or "If I were a color, I would be . . ."
2. Have people tell a little bit about their choice. However, "I don't know, I just liked it!" is an okay response.
3. Let your imagination be your guide for other analogies.

Intermediate

These exercises are appropriate for groups that know each other by name and are comfortable with each other. They require some risking as the sharing moves deeper to issues and values. The following examples are from *Value Certification: A Handbook of Practical Strategies for Teachers and Students,* by S. Simon (1972):

Examples

Value Clarification: Forced Choices:

1. If people are able, have them physically move to a designated spot to indicate their choice. If mobility is limited, people can indicate their choice by a show of hands.
2. Read statements such as: "Are you more of a saver or a spender?" "Are you more like New York City or Colorado?" "Are you more like a rose or a daisy?"
3. Allow participants time to share why they made the choice they did. Remember, "just 'cause" is an okay answer!

Value Clarification: Twenty Things You Love to Do–any size group:

1. Make a list of 20 things you love to do.
2. Put a dollar sign ($) by those that take money.
3. Put a letter "A" by those that you prefer to do alone and a letter "P" by those you prefer to do with other people.
4. Pick your top five (5).

5. Put the date you last did those top five.
6. In groups of 3 or 4, share your list and anything you learned from doing it.

Sharing Joys and concerns: good for starting meetings: Go around the table or room and ask each person to share a joy *and* a sorrow. It is a good idea if the leader goes first to model and to give others a chance to think. Also, remember that "I pass" is an okay response.

Going Deeper

These exercises are the riskiest of all and work best in groups that have been together for a while and feel very comfortable with each other. The rule of confidentiality should be frequently mentioned. A non-judgmental atmosphere will promote honest sharing of feelings and thoughts. The group should not be larger than 10-12 persons.

Examples

Serendipity Bible:[2] The *Serendipity Bible* is designed for small group Bible study. The Biblical text is surrounded with marginal notes that encourage the exploration of one's own feelings and thoughts.

Study Series Designed Around Books: There are many books that are designed for group study with suggested exercises and questions at the end of each chapter. One such book is *The Enduring Heart: Spirituality for the Long Haul,* by W. Au (2000), Mahwah: Paulist Press. Other books many be available from denominational book stores.

Bible Studies Series: Many denominations offer Bible Study Series that contain not only Biblical background information but also suggestions of ways to make the study interactive.

Spiritual Life Reviews: Richard Morgan reminds us that "a spiritual life review not only helps people embrace their past history, it provides a real challenge as to what to include in the rest of life" (Morgan, 1996, 31). There are several excellent resources[3] to use in a group setting for spiritual life review or guided autobiography. One is *Remembering Your Story: A Guide to Spiritual Autobiography,* by Richard L. Morgan, which comes with a leader's guide.

WHERE CAN WE DO COMMUNITY BUILDING?

As noted earlier, the church is a gathering place and each of those gathering times offers an opportunity for community. Even a cursory glance shows us many possibilities:

- *Worship service*–How about sharing a joy from the past week along with our name during the "greeting moments"?
- *After worship fellowship*–How about a "treasure hunt"? Find someone with your same birth month or birth state or who likes the same flavor of ice cream or . . .
- *Pot luck dinner*–How about a birthday theme? Everyone sits at the table (appropriately decorated, of course) for their birthday month. Or if your group is comfortable enough, line up by age. Your newcomers will feel more involved when everyone is given a "sharing topic" and your long-time members may even discover things they didn't know about each other!
- *Religious Education classes*–Depending on the comfort level of the class, there are important questions to be pondered about how we live as God's people in our world. Using the guidelines for community building can help people feel safer about sharing their joys, doubts, successes, and struggles of their personal faith journey.
- *Choir*–Ever think about sharing what your favorite piece of music is? Or maybe an early musical memory?
- *Board, committee meetings*–Begin with some kind of sharing, such as: What made you glad to be alive this past week? Or what is one hope you have for your congregation?
- *Service projects*–Make sure that people working together, whether it is in a "soup kitchen" or a Habitat for Humanity project or any other service project, know each other's names. A step to "going deeper" might be a gathering after the project work for sharing about the experience: What was good? What was difficult? Where did you sense God at work?

The list could go on and you could add many more possibilities in your particular setting. Just remember that wherever two or three are gathered, there is an opportunity for community building.

A FINAL WORD

As you have read many of the things in this chapter, you have probably been saying to yourself "We already do that!" And you are absolutely right! The fact is that one of the things we do in the church is build community, and you can enhance and build on what you already do.

Is it to be hoped that now your eyes have been opened to some new setting where you can continue building that community. Your mind has been challenged to think about ways to expand and deepen the sense of community. Your soul is excited about possibilities for engagement with others around you.

May God bless your continued journey of belonging!

NOTES

1. From the Web site of Tree Bressen *www.treegroup.info*
2. Serendipity Bibles in several translations are available from *ZondervanBible.com*
3. See resource pages at end of chapter.

REFERENCES

Cummings, E., & Henry, W. (1990). Growing old. As quoted in D. K. Harris (Ed.), *Sociology of Aging*. New York: Harper & Row.

Harris, D. K. (1990). *Sociology of aging*. New York: Harper & Row.

Johnson, B. (1989). Spirituality and the later years. *Journal of Religion & Aging, 6*(3/4), 126.

McClellan, A. (1989). What my pastor needs to know about me. *Southwestern Journal of Theology, 31*(Summer).

Moberg, D. O. (2001). The spiritual life review. In D. O. Moberg (Ed.), *Aging and Spirituality: Spiritual Dimensions of Aging Theory, Research, Practice, and Policy* (Vol. Chapter 12, pp. 162-166). Binghamton: The Haworth Press, Inc.

Morgan, R. L. (1996). *Remembering your story: A guide to spiritual autobiography*. Nashville: Upper Room Press.

Row, J. W., & Kahn, R. L. (1998). *Successful Aging*. New York: Pantheon Books.

Simon, S. (1972). *Value clarification: A handbook of practical strategies for teachers and students*. New York: A Hart Book.

RESOURCES

Basic Exercises

Your own imagination may be your best resource. Just ask yourself what would it be fun for us to share with each other.

www.treegroup.info click on "toolbox"

Typing in the words "get acquainted exercises" or "icebreakers" in an Internet search engine will produce a number of resources most of which are directed toward students or business meetings but which adapt well to church settings. A recent search of "Yahoo" produced the following among the results:

www.muohio.edu/studentactivities/handout/breaktheice.html

www.wholeperson.com

Intermediate Exercises

Larson, R. S., & Larson, D. E. (1976). *Values and faith.* Minneapolis: Winston Press. This book is out of print, but *www.amazon.com* has several available.
Simon, S. (1972). *Value clarification: A handbook of practical strategies for teachers and students.* New York: A Hart Book.
Note: This and several other Value Clarification books, some in-print and some out-of-print are available from *www.amazon.com.* Type in "value clarification" and search.

Going Deeper

Au, W. (2000). *The enduring heart: Spirituality for the long haul.* Mahwah: Paulist Press.
Birren, J., & Cochran, K. (2001). *Telling the stories of life through guided autobiography groups.* Baltimore: Johns Hopkins University Press.
Birren, J. E., & Deutchman, D. E. (1991). *Guiding autobiography groups for older adults.* Baltimore: Johns Hopkins University Press.
Journey Through the Bible, a Bible Study series published by Cokesbury (800-672-1789). This series, which covers every book in the Bible, contains not only good Biblical background information, but also several suggestions in each lesson to encourage interaction of the participants. Each volume includes a leader's guide and student's book.
Morgan, R. L. (1996). *Remembering your story: A guide to spiritual autobiography.* Nashville: Upper Room Press. A Leader's Guide is also available.
Serendipity Bible is available in several translations from *www.zondervan.com*

Recommended Reading

Carlson, D. (1997). *Engaging in ministry with older adults.* Herndon: Alban Institute Publications.

Coleman, L. (1989). Ministering to the aged. *Southwestern Journal of Theology,* *31*(Summer), 5-51.

Harris, D. K. (1990). *Sociology of aging.* New York: Harper & Row.

Johnson, B. (1989). Spirituality and the later years. *Journal of Religion & Aging, 6*(3/4), 126.

Kollar, N. (1985). Towards a spirituality of aging and old age. *Journal of Religion & Aging, 1*(3), 49-59.

McClellan, A. (1989). What my pastor needs to know about me. *Southwestern Journal of Theology, 31*(Summer), 23.

Moberg, D. O. (Ed.). (2001). *Aging and spirituality: Spiritual dimensions of aging theory, research, practice, and policy.* Binghamton: The Haworth Press, Inc.

Moberg, D. O. (1989). Spirituality and aging: Challenges on the frontier of gerontology. *Southwestern Journal of Theology, 31*(Summer), 12-21.

Morgan, R. L. (1996). Remembering your story: A guide to spiritual autobiography. Nashville: Upper Room Press.

Row, J. W., & Kahn, R. L. (1998). *Successful aging.* New York: Pantheon Books.

Simon, S. (1972). *Value clarification: A handbook of practical strategies for teachers and students.* 1990: Hadley, MA: Values Press.

PART THREE:
PUTTING IT ALL TOGETHER

Building Blocks
for Older Adult Ministry

Donald R. Koepke, MDiv, BCC

SUMMARY. The final building block is deciding what program fits ministry goals, congregational resources and skills, and the needs of the older adults who will benefit from this ministry. A final form is used to choose, from the many options gathered in the previous steps, which ministries to begin, at this time, for this group of people, with these specific resources, be they congregational resources or those from community collaboration. Choosing target dates for specific tasks and assigning those tasks to specific committee member is crucial for success. The place of attendance in declaring success or failure is discussed. Using the OAM mission statement as a basis for continuing evaluation is suggested. *[Article copies available for a fee from The Haworth Document Delivery Service: 1-800-HAWORTH. E-mail address: <docdelivery@haworthpress. com> Website: <http://www.HaworthPress.com> © 2005 by The Haworth Press, Inc. All rights reserved.]*

[Haworth co-indexing entry note]: "Building Blocks for Older Adult Ministry." Koepke, Donald R. Co-published simultaneously in *Journal of Religion, Spirituality & Aging* (The Haworth Pastoral Press, an imprint of The Haworth Press, Inc.) Vol. 17, No. 3/4, 2005, pp. 169-195; and: *Ministering to Older Adults: The Building Blocks* (ed: Donald R. Koepke) The Haworth Pastoral Press, an imprint of The Haworth Press, Inc., 2005, pp. 169-195. Single or multiple copies of this article are available for a fee from The Haworth Document Delivery Service [1-800-HAWORTH, 9:00 a.m. - 5:00 p.m. (EST). E-mail address: docdelivery@ haworthpress.com].

Available online at http://www.haworthpress.com/web/JRSA
2005 by The Haworth Press, Inc. All rights reserved.
doi:10.1300/J496v17n03_12

KEYWORDS. Focused ministry, centrality of mission statements, simplicity, target dates, evaluation

We are finally at the end of our journey: the task of putting together all of what has been decided and formulating an initial plan of ministry. Each of the steps of this planning process has been important. One block builds upon the other until a refreshing, vital, focused plan arises.

So far, we have decided Who are the Elderly? Who are the recipients of our ministry? Again, everyone on a planning committee has a different opinion that has been developed throughout a lifetime by personal reading, thinking and experience. It is crucial that a committee comes to a consensus on the question "Who are the Elderly?" even if this target group changes as the ministry is implemented and evaluated. Older Adult Ministries are best when they are intentional.

Second, we have decided what the outcome of our ministry needs to be. Through prayer and study, as well as discussion and even debate, it is essential that planning committees agree on the basic direction (purpose) of the ministry. Otherwise the ministry might be intentional but it will not be focused.

Third, there has been an evaluation of congregational readiness from two perspectives. First were identified existing ministries. Second, the infrastructure of the decision-making process within your congregation was noted. Successful ministries grow out of present congregational culture and goals. Successful ministries have roots.

Finally, guided by the Older Adult Ministry Planning Grid, you explored the five categories of a successful older adult ministry. It is to be hoped that, after reading the chapters of Part Two, your planning grid is filled with ministries or ministry ideas that came to mind as you read. Successful ministries are resourced.

Now it is time to put it all together.

THE PLANNING GRID AS A DREAM

The Planning Grid (Appendix G, page 191) is an expression of a dream. It is an expression of how you would like your ministry to be if you had unlimited time and unlimited resources. Except for large, mature programs, few Older Adult Ministries will succeed in being "all things to all people." Every program category is important. Every ministry group is crucial but your congregation may not have the resources to provide every ministry to every person. Therefore, you need to decide on a place to start. That starting place might not be where your congregation's ministry ultimately ends. As you begin a ministry and evaluate the effectiveness of that ministry, goals will change. New perspectives will be discovered. Even greater needs will be exposed than were seen initially but the important thing is to start someplace. The chart in Appendix I (page 193) is designed to help in this process.

Begin Where You Are

Start by reaffirming who your target group is going to be. No groups are more worthy than another but a decision has to be made. I would suggest that you select by circling no more than two of the four ministry groups (active, transitional, frail, caregivers). If you are beginning your ministry from scratch, it might even be better to decide on only one ministry group! How is that decision made?

Look at the planning grid. Note the ministries that are already present within your congregation. Are there any glaring deficiencies? Any present strengths? How do these insights affect your decision about the initial target group? Are there many ministries (although perhaps not enough) directed towards the frail? Some congregations already have a Stephen's Ministry or a program of volunteer visitation of the sick. Does that fact make you think that perhaps your target group should be the transitional and not the frail?

At the same time, if your congregation already has an "adequate" ministry toward the frail (tape ministry, telephone partners, etc.), perhaps it would be a logical step to further develop ministry with caregivers. Remember, one of the keys to a successful OAM is that the ministry is rooted in the existing congregational culture. Perhaps your congregation has always been a "family" who has "taken care of its own," and thus providing basic resources and education in caregiving might be a great place to begin your OAM, a "slam-dunk" winner.

Or else, your grid might suggest that while there are enough resources for other groups that the active elderly lack attention, needing to be treated as being more than the worker bees of the congregation. Perhaps their spiritual life can be deepened if the congregation would sponsor a life review group where participants track the hand of God in their lives, strengthening the spiritual bond and preparing the active elder for the challenges of loss that, if they live long enough, are sure to come. While sheer numbers might not be the only perspective from which to make a target-group decision, the greatest number of people with a need that can be managed by the resources of your congregation might be a starting point.

Decide on a Programmatic Direction

I believe that a congregation is able to begin no more than three new ministries at any one time without becoming burned out in the process. Therefore, the second section of Appendix A asks that the planning committee "rank order" the five categories of older adult ministry determining which category is most important, second most important, third most important and so forth. Since all the categories are important a different measure than mere interest must be used.

Avoid discussing specific ministries for one more moment. Instead, which ministry category, according to a consensus of the committee, is most important *at this time?* Of course they all are important but a new ministry can't do everything all at once.

Begin this task by identifying the strengths of your congregation. One of the ways that a congregation can discern the direction that God wants it to take is to assess the resources that the members bring to the table. A congregation with a group of former nurses might be able to begin a vital visitation ministry with the frail. A congregation with connections to the community might be able to enlist people in providing service outside of their own needs. A congregation with a retired teacher might have the ability to begin a strong educational ministry. Congregations that are strong in worship or prayer might see an added emphasis in spiritual development blossom. It is not helpful to plant oak trees in the middle of the desert. It might be more advantageous to plant cacti or bougainvillea. Where and what are your strengths as a congregation? What is the cultural climate of your congregation? What values have been important over the years? These questions might give a clue as to the ministry category with which to begin. The answers will provide the soil which will nourish the ministries you plant.

At the same time, resources that are lacking within the congregation can be gained through collaboration with like-minded churches or community organizations. A congregation with lots of frail elderly and caregivers might see a need for a grief support group. Lacking an experienced and trained leader, they might be able to link up with a local hospice organization that is in need of a site for a new group. A congregation that has but a few active elders interested in a retreat on the spirituality of aging might join with enough local congregations until the number of participants to form a viable retreat group is secured. A congregation that wishes to sponsor a time of worship and fellowship (food is always good) for transitional persons who are having difficulty getting to church on Sundays might augment congregational volunteer drivers by coordinating their efforts with a local dial-a-ride organization. Churches that are limited in cash can seek a partnership with a senior center or their Area Agency on Aging.

Remember, a congregation's resources are far greater than what the members themselves possess. There are community organizations with common values and goals that are more than willing to join forces and improve the outreach of both organizations. During the planning process is not the time to be timid but to be bold and creative, prayerful, and attentive to all of the possibilities that God places in our midst.

Now choose two or three programs from the boxes in the planning grid that fit your needs. This is the time to discuss specific programs and ministries. This is the time for each person to advocate for the ministry(s) closest to the heart. Keep talking until a consensus that includes two or three possibilities emerges.

Use Desired Outcomes to Evaluate Your Decisions

Programmatic decisions, as I have often said in this journal, are not to be made because a committee likes a particular program or because the resources are readily available. The true litmus test for any older adult ministry is whether or not that ministry is consistent with the congregation's mission statement. Thus, the third section of the planning guide (Appendix I, page 193) asks "How does this starting point fulfill your mission statement?" Review your mission statement that describes the desired outcomes of your OAM. How does your chosen target group, as well as the possible programmatic area(s), lead your congregation closer to fulfilling its stated goals and purposes? This is the time to be specific and challenging rather than philosophical.

A simple method of completing this portion of the form might be to copy the essential phrases of your mission statement onto a piece of paper. Then, write two or three sentences describing how and why each phrase is fulfilled by what you plan to do. This task is not mere busy work. You are exploring the potential effects of the ministries that you have identified and whether or not those effects are consistent with your intentions. This is no different from a teacher's lesson objectives or a business executive's monthly goal. How can you evaluate your efforts if you haven't clearly articulated your goals? No one wants to find success with a great ministry only to discover that it didn't meet the needs of people.

Establish Target Dates

Now is the time to be really specific. For each ministry selected, develop a set of target dates that will lead to its successful birth. If one of ministries that you have identified is to begin a lecture series on older adult issues, then what needs to be done and in what order for this dream to become a reality? If you hope to begin a telephone buddy system for frail and transitional persons, what are the steps that must happen to gain support for such a ministry? Who is going to be responsible for each task? When is each task projected to be completed? Target dates are simply that: targets. Unforeseen circumstances can always arise that make completing a task on time impossible, but that should not stop a planning committee from making realistic projections for the completion of the various elements in the plan.

Begin by writing down the date that you would like to begin the ministry. Note what needs to be done between now and the opening date and in what order? When? Depending on the specific ministry, some of the items you might want to include are:

- Identify person(s) to be responsible for program development
- If needed, recruit additional persons to be on task group
- What resources are needed for the success of the ministry?
    - From within the Congregation?
    - From outside the congregation (like special speakers)?
    - What written resources are needed?
- Who are the intended participants?
    - Will community persons be welcomed? Invited?
- How are you going to publicize the event?
    - Who is going to write the newsletter article or the text of the special letter? The article for the local newspaper? Speakers at "announcement time" at worship?
- Coordination with other congregational events?
- Is approval needed from a board or committee?
- Sign-up/pre-registration?
- Room set up? Refreshments?
- Identification of host for any guest presenters

Appendix J (page 194) describes the development planning for three ministries: the beginning of a group for older adults in the congregation called The OWLs (Older Wiser Lutherans) in four months, a life review class two months later, and bereavement training through a community organization (AARP) in nine months. A one-year anniversary retreat was tentatively scheduled in order to insure evaluation of the effectiveness of these ministries and plan for the second year. The committee had five members (plus the pastor) at its first meeting. Note how some ministries (newsletter articles, worship announcements, sermon series on Aging and Spirituality) were able to start quickly while others were delayed.

Attendance Is Not Always the Best Indicator of Success

It is important to note that the number of attendees might not be the best way to evaluate the effectiveness of your older adult ministry. Over the years, I have observed that the more that is expected from participants, the smaller the ministry group tends to be. Everyone seems to come out for the annual Christmas party, but the number of persons involved in the contemplative prayer group might be comparatively small. Yet the depths of spiritual growth and insight might be greater for the small contemplative prayer group than for the large Christmas celebration. However, each group has its place in a developed older adult ministry.

There is a place for the large group that does not ask much of its participants. Not everyone is ready for the intimate, high-commitment group that explores the value of spiritual direction in later life. At the same time, there will be some persons who will be quickly bored by playing bingo all the time. Effective Older Adult Ministries are those that provide a continuum of ever deepening experiences that, step-by-step, draw people ever closer to what is the ultimate goal of OAM, intimacy with God and with the Body of Christ, the Church.

The design of an effective Older Adult Ministry can be likened to a target used in archery. Like an archery target, the center might be the smallest but its value is the greatest. Like an archery target, the outer rings might be larger and easier to hit but are of the least value. Large groups (lunch and a speaker) are valuable in that they allow new persons to enter the ministry without a lot of personal exposure or commitment. Small groups (support groups, discussion groups about personal faith goals, etc.) are also important in that they provide a place for people who want to go deeper. Groups in the middle (Bible studies, retreats,

Alpha groups, etc.) provide a bridge between the two. The basic principle is simple: a continuum of ministry for a continuum of persons.

The Need for Ongoing Evaluation

Quality Older Adult Ministries evaluate everything that is done for their effectiveness in fulfilling the mission statement as well as to learn how more effectively to provide the same ministry in the future. A congregational Older Adult Ministry is never complete, always growing, continually searching and, thus, always fun to organize and be a part of. Note that the example target date chart (Appendix J) provides a time for evaluation.

- How did we do?
- Were our goals accomplished? (Review your mission statement)
- What was learned?
- How can the ministry be improved?

A Final Word

Older Adult Ministry is not merely a ministry with older adults. It is an opportunity to gain an insight into life, for the spiritual issues of the elderly are really no different from the issues of those who are younger. The spiritual issues of the elderly are the basic human issues: Who am I? Why am I? What has it all meant? Where is everything heading? Is my faith in God enough to fill my needs or do I require sturdy legs or healthy eyes or a job? Am I worthy in and of myself or do I need to accomplish, create, produce in order to be of worth? If I can't remember because of dementia or disability am I diminished as a human being? These are human questions, spiritual questions. An Older Adult Ministry allows people to peek into the final chapter of life and see life as it is, not as we want it to be. The issues of the elderly are not different from when they were younger but now that they are older, many of the distractions have been taken from them. The reality that one is human is continually a part of the life of older people.

Older Adult Ministry. What an opportunity to learn, to grow, to experience life.

Appendices

APPENDIX A. Building Blocks for Older Adult Ministry

BUILDING BLOCK NUMBER ONE: WHO ARE THE ELDERLY?

In 1900, 4% of population were age 65 and over (1 out of 25 or 3 million). Today 13% are over 65 (1 out of 8 or 35 million which is more than Canada). Middle projection of Bureau of Census: By 2040 25% will be 65 and over.

Today, 4 out of every 5 people live to age 70.

Beginning in 1996: 10,000 Americans turn age 50 every day. Every year, for the next 20 years, 1 million will reach age 65.

One-half to 2/3 of all the persons who have ever reached age 65 are living today.

Life Expectancy:
> In 1900, life expectancy was 45.
> Today, life expectancy is 80.
> If today is your 65th birthday you can expect 17 more years (or about 20% of life-time).

Fastest growing segment of today's society are those over age 85.
> By 2050 those over 85 will be 50% of those over 65.
> By 2050 80-year-olds will outnumber 5-year-olds.

Between 1980 and today the number of persons over 100 has doubled. By 2050 it is estimated that 1.1 million will be age 100 or over.

Implication:
> Today, one out of five persons has a dementia.
>> At age 85, one out of every two persons has dementia.
> Today, there are 4 million people with Alzheimers.
>> By 2050, there will be 14 million persons with Alzheimers.
> The need for caregiving doubles every five years beyond age 65.

Ninety percent of all caregiving is provided by family members.

APPENDIX B. Who Are the Elderly in your Congregation?

Church Name_____

1. What is the Total Membership of your Congregation? _____

2. How many persons in your congregation are in the following groups?

Active Elderly	Raw_____	Percentage of Total_____
Frail Elderly	Raw_____	Percentage of Total_____
Transitional	Raw_____	Percentage of Total_____
Caregivers	Raw_____	Percentage of Total_____

3. Special membership needs:

Transportation	Raw———	Percentage of Total———
Extra Visitation	Raw———	Percentage of Total———
Special Assistance	Raw———	Percentage of Total———
Home-Centered Ministry	Raw———	Percentage of Total———

4. How many older adults live within the zip code of your church? See www.factfinder.census.gov

5. Note any characteristics of the older adults in your community, i.e., age, income, number of households with one occupant, occupation, own, or rent, etc. www.factfinder.census.gov

6. Has your congregation ever actively and intentionally sought to evangelize older adults within your community?

                                                                    Yes   No

What were the effects of this decision on your community?

Appendix C. Hopes and Dreams as an Expression of Mission

Writing a Mission Statement

- **What do we want to accomplish?**
- **What is the standard that we will evaluate present ministry and guide the development of future ministry?**

Step One: List as many ministry outcomes that you can think of in five minutes

1.

2.

3.

4.

5.

6.

Step Two: Rank the goals above in order of importance, 1, 2, 3, etc.

Step Three: Circle the essential words in each ministry goal.

Step Four: Based on the above steps, write below a simple, declarative sentence that describes your hopes and dreams for your older adult ministry.

APPENDIX D. Assess Existing Ministry

Church Name_____

Church Address_____

1. What is the Total Membership of your Congregation? _____

2. How many persons in your congregation are in the following groups?

   Active Elderly   Raw_____   Percentage of Total_____
   Frail Elderly   Raw_____   Percentage of Total_____
   Transitional   Raw_____   Percentage of Total_____
   Caregivers   Raw_____   Percentage of Total_____

3. What percentage of your membership needs.

   Transportation _____   Extra Visitation _____
   Special Assistance _____   Home-Centered Ministry _____

4. Do you have a social group especially for older adults? Yes   No

   If yes, is it run by: Themselves _____ Others_____

5. Do you have a group of volunteers to drive people to clinics, dentists, shopping, etc.?
   Yes No
   If yes, what is the age group of most of the volunteers _____

6. Does your church have the following:
   (a) Tape recordings of church services for the home centered? _____
   (b) Ramp Access to Sanctuary _____
   (c) Ramp Access to Social Hall _____
   (d) Ramp Access to classrooms _____
   (e) Wheelchair accessible restrooms _____
   (f) Pull bars in restroom stalls _____
   (g) Access to altar by wheelchairs/walkers _____
   (h) Bright lighting in sanctuary/social hall_____
   (i) Blank wall in back of altar/pulpit _____
   (j) Hearing Assist equipment_____
   (k) Place for wheelchairs prominently in sanctuary _____
   (l) Worship Materials in large print _____

(m) Meals on Wheels _____

(n) Home Repair services _____

(o) Home Chore Service _____

(p) Parish Nurse Program _____

(q) Stephen's Ministry (or similar) _____

(r) Exercise/Aerobics classes for older adults _____

(s) Cooking and Nutrition Classes for older adults _____

(t) Respite Care Relievers Program _____

(u) Telephone Reassurance Program _____

(v) Adult Day Care Center _____

(w) Prayer/Concern Chains _____

(x) Emergency Hot-Line _____

(y) Support Groups _____ List: _____

(z) Older Adult Service Recognition Program _____

7. Approximately how many older adults are doing volunteer work in your church?
   _____total hours per week ____ month ____ year ____

8. Do any of your organizations organize trips, movies, parties or other events for older adults? Describe:

9. Does your church minister to the needs of persons in your community who are not church members or attenders?

10. Do you have volunteers who visit older persons in the hospital _____
    Home centered _____ Nursing Home _____

11. Are older adults represented on the governing board of your church or other committees of your church? _____

12. Does your church offer classes/seminars for older adults in any of the following:
    (a) Grief and loss _____
    (b) Spiritual Development _____
    (c) Death and Dying _____
    (d) Marriage Communication _____
    (e) Retirement Planning _____
    (f) Caregiving _____
    (g) How to choose a retirement community/nursing home _____

13. Do older adults participate in the following ministries?
- a. Local church teaching ministries?

  For children _____

  For youth _____

  For young adults _____

  For Middle Aged _____

  For Older Adults _____
- b. After school Latchkey Programs for Children _____
- c. Preschool volunteer or employee _____
- d. Telephone Reassurance Program _____
- e. Serve in Worship Areas:

  Ushers _____

  Greeters _____

  Lay Assistants (Liturgists) _____

  Readers _____

  Choir _____

  Song Leader _____

  Soloists _____

- f. Church office assistance:

  Bulletins/Worship materials _____

  Newsletters _____

  Directories _____

  Mailings _____

  Receptionist _____

  Volunteer (or paid) office assistant _____

- g. Other areas: _____

Adapted from: Local Church Program Assessment
"Designing A Ministry By, With, and For Older Adults"
Richard H. Gentzler, Jr.
Printed with permission

APPENDIX E. Creating a Successful Elder Ministry Evaluation Form

1. Our program is intentional, planned, and focused

1   2   3   4   5   6   7
Not Yet ☹   ☺ Doing It Well

Why this evaluation?

How we are going to improve?

2. Our program has a sense of rootedness

1   2   3   4   5   6   7
Not Yet ☹   ☺ Doing It Well

Why this evaluation?

How we are going to improve?

3. Our program is based on demonstrated needs

1   2   3   4   5   6   7
Not Yet ☹   ☺ Doing It Well

Why this evaluation?

How we are going to improve?

4. Our program is enhanced by good record keeping and accountability

1	2	3	4	5	6	7
Not Yet ☹						☺ Doing It Well

Why this evaluation?

How we are going to improve?

5. Our program has identifiable leadership

1	2	3	4	5	6	7
Not Yet ☹						☺ Doing It Well

Why this evaluation?

How we are going to improve?

6. Our program has leaders trained in gerontology

1	2	3	4	5	6	7
Not Yet ☹						☺ Doing It Well

Why this evaluation?

How we are going to improve?

7. Our program has the support of the church council

1	2	3	4	5	6	7
Not Yet ☹						☺ Doing It Well

Why this evaluation?

How we are going to improve?

8. Our program communicates well with the congregation

1	2	3	4	5	6	7
Not Yet ☹   ☺ Doing It Well

Why this evaluation?

How we are going to improve?

9. Our program communicates well with the community

1	2	3	4	5	6	7
Not Yet ☹   ☺ Doing It Well

Why this evaluation?

How we are going to improve?

10. Our program is supported by a strong physical infrastructure

1	2	3	4	5	6	7
Not Yet ☹   ☺ Doing It Well

Why this evaluation?

How we are going to improve?

11. Our program has adequate financial and volunteer support

1	2	3	4	5	6	7

Not Yet ☹   ☺ Doing It Well

Why this evaluation?

How we are going to improve?

12. Our program is blessed with community ties

1	2	3	4	5	6	7

Not Yet ☹   ☺ Doing It Well

Why this evaluation?

How we are going to improve?

13. Our program is based on neighborliness and inter-congregational cooperation

1	2	3	4	5	6	7

Not Yet ☹   ☺ Doing It Well

Why this evaluation?

How we are going to improve?

14. Our program intentionally addresses the spiritual needs of the people whom we serve

1	2	3	4	5	6	7

Not Yet ☹   ☺ Doing It Well

Why this evaluation?

How are we going to improve?

APPENDIX F

Name:_____ Date: _____

I feel as though I belong to the congregational family
I believe that the following can help with my sense of belonging
___ Myself
___ My family
___ Church Members
___ My Minister
___ Community Organizations

It would expand my feeling of belonging if I were to receive:

1	2	3	4	5	6	7
Definitely						Not Really

___ Occasional Flowers from the Altar
___ Worship Bulletin each week
___ Regular visits by church members
___ Occasional visits by Pastoral Staff
___ Regular visits by church members (Stephen's Ministers, Elders, Deacons)
___ Received a daily telephone contact from another church member
___ I had a volunteer task that I was able to perform
___ Made a daily telephone contact to another church member
___ Had assistance in gaining skills in intercessory prayer
___ Had transportation to worship
___ Had transportation to small group meetings (Specify:_____)
___ Had help with simple home maintenance, chores, meal preparation
___ Remembered by the congregation in prayer
___ Other:

I feel connected with God:

1	2	3	4	5	6	7
Definitely						Not Really

I believe that the following can help with my connection with God

____ Myself

____ My family

____ Church Friends

____ Church members (Visitation Group, Stephen Ministers, etc).

____ My Minister

____ Community Organizations (Specify:_____)

I might be assisted in my connection with God if I were to receive:

1	2	3	4	5	6	7
Definitely						Not Really

____ Holy Communion (How Often: _____)

____ Assistance in my prayer life

____ audiotapes of Sunday Worship

____ access to daily devotional books

____ access to Inspirational Books

____ a small support group met in my home

____ someone to share hopes, fears, struggles

____ help in helping others

____ Other:

At this time in my life, I am continuing to learn and grow.

1	2	3	4	5	6	7
Definitely						Not Really

____ Myself

____ My family

____ Church Friends

____ Church members (Visitation Group, Stephen Ministers, etc).

____ My Minister

____ Community Organizations (Specify:_____)

It would expand my learning and growing in God if I were to receive:

____ Audio or Video Tapes of sermons and classes held at church

____ Interesting and stimulating books to read

____ Access to religious books on tape

___ I were involved in the life of someone younger than I (i.e., mentoring)
___ My skills were still useful to the church (Specify skill_____)
___ Contact with someone with whom I could share my faith
___ A small monthly study group met in my home
___ Other

I have help with my doubts and struggles about my faith

1	2	3	4	5	6	7
Definitely						Not Really

I believe that the following can help with my doubts and struggles

___Myself   ___Church Friends   ___Church Members
___My Family   ___My Minister   (Visitation Group)
___Community Organizations (Specify:_____)

It would help my efforts to deal with doubts and struggles if I were to receive:
___ visits from members of the church
___ visits from my minister so we can talk about important things
___ the intercessory prayers of others
___ transportation to church functions (Specifiy:_____)
___ help in seeing beyond my personal situation
___ an enhanced Christian understanding of suffering
___ opportunities to serve others to the best of my abilities
___ Other:

I would like to suggest the following for enhancing the spiritual care of persons connected with our church:

1.

2.

3.

4.

The following hinders my relationship with the congregational family:

___ NO HINDRANCES

___Diificulty with vision   ___Difficulty reading

___Difficulty hearing   ___Can't remember names

___No friends   ___Can't sit long enough

___Difficulty walking   ___Too many stairs

___No location for wheelchair   ___Worship materials too small

___Medical reasons   ___Lost interest in being among

___Caregiving Responsibilities   people

___Personal issues that might embarrass me in public

Assessment made by:_____

APPENDIX G. Program Planning Tool

Mission Statement:

	Spiritual Development	Continued Learning	Opportunities to Serve	Opportunities to Be Served	Community Building
Active					
Transitional					
Frail					
Caregivers					

APPENDIX H. Program Planning Tool

Mission Statement: The Elder Ministry Program of First UMC is to be a ministry by, with, and for older adults within and beyond the walls of our church. we shall continue to offer and deepen programs and services that will mediate the love and care of God, responding in new ways to the needs, hurts,and hopes of older adults.

	Spiritual Development	Continued Learning	Opportunities to Serve	Opportunities to Be Served	Community Building
Active	**Autobiography Class **Searchlight Class **Pathfinders Class	**Autobiography Class **Searchlight Class **Pathfinders Class	**Care Ministry **Worship Leaders		**Searchlight Class **Pathfinders Class
Transitional					
Frail	**Tape Ministry			**Telephone Ministry	
Caregivers					

APPENDIX I. Target Dates

With the knowledge that there is always more that can and should be done in older adult ministry within our congregation, we propose to begin as follows:

The Who (Circle all appropriate target groups for initial ministry)

Active	Transitional	Frail	Caregivers
Elders	Elders	Elders	

The What (Rank Order the Ministry Categories in order of importance)

___Spiritual Development
___Learning Opportunities
___Service Opportunity
___Service Provision
___Community Building

The Why (How does this starting point fulfill your mission statement)

The When (use the following time line to describe how the ministry will unfold (or develop your own)

NOTE ON THE TIME LINE

<u>Ministry</u>   **WHO** <u>Responsible</u>

Immediately:

One Month

Two Months

Three Months

Six Months

Nine Months

One Year

**WHEN THE NEXT PHASE (S) OF MINISTRY
ARE TARGETED TO BEGIN
(You may wish to make out a Target Dates form
for each new Ministry)**

APPENDIX J. Target Dates

With the knowledge that there is always more that can and should be done in older adult ministry within our congregation, we propose to begin as follows:

The Who (Circle all appropriate target groups for initial ministry)

Active	**Transitional**	Frail	Caregivers
Elders	**Elders**	Elders	

The What (Rank Order the Ministry Categories in order of importance)

__1_Spiritual Development
__2_Learning Opportunities
__3_Service Opportunity
__4_Service Provision
__5_Social Interaction

The Why (How does this starting point fulfill your mission statement)

1. The majority of our members fall into the Active and Transitional. We need to get people to stop thinking that Elder Ministry is ministry to the frail exclusively. 2. We need to gain more volunteer strength. 3. We need to begin developing relationships with groups outside of church. 4. We need to begin to develop a better view of aging by congregation.

The When (use the following time line to describe how the ministry will unfold (or develop your own)

	Ministry	**WHO** Responsible
Immediately:	Make presentation to Council Begin Worship Announcements	George Pastor/Sally
One Month	Newsletter Articles re: Aging Contact CSEA for Assistance	George, Pastor
Two Months	Planning for Beginning Ministry (Recruit Additional help) Sermon Series on Aging/Spirituality	George, Sally, Pastor, Theresa, Pastor

	Ministry	WHO Responsible
Three Months	Planning for Beginning Ministry	George, Sally, Theresa
	Recruit OWL leadership	
Four Months	Older, Wiser Lutherans	Sally, Pete, Theresa
	Kick Off Luncheon	
	Contact ALZ. Assn. for Speaker	
Six Months	Begin Life Review Class (Inter-Congregational)	George
Nine Months	Invite AARP to train Bereavement	Theresa
	Bereavement Befriender classes	
One Year	Evaluation Retreat	

**NOTE ON THE TIME LINE
WHEN THE NEXT PHASE (S) OF MINISTRY
ARE TARGETED TO BEGIN
(You may wish to make out a Target Dates form
for each new Ministry)**

Index

BOOK ORDER FORM!

Order a copy of this book with this form or online at:
http://www.haworthpress.com/store/product.asp?sku=5687

Ministering to Older Adults
The Building Blocks

____ in softbound at $22.95 ISBN-13: 978-0-7890-3049-8 / ISBN-10: 0-7890-3049-7.
____ in hardbound at $39.95 ISBN-13: 978-0-7890-3048-1 / ISBN-10: 0-7890-3048-9.

COST OF BOOKS _____

POSTAGE & HANDLING _____
US: $4.00 for first book & $1.50
for each additional book
Outside US: $5.00 for first book
& $2.00 for each additional book.

SUBTOTAL _____

In Canada: add 7% GST. _____

STATE TAX _____
CA, IL, IN, MN, NJ, NY, OH, PA & SD residents
please add appropriate local sales tax.

FINAL TOTAL _____
If paying in Canadian funds, convert
using the current exchange rate,
UNESCO coupons welcome.

❑ BILL ME LATER:
Bill-me option is good on US/Canada/
Mexico orders only; not good to jobbers,
wholesalers, or subscription agencies.

❑ Signature _____

❑ Payment Enclosed: $ _____

❑ PLEASE CHARGE TO MY CREDIT CARD:
❑ Visa ❑ MasterCard ❑ AmEx ❑ Discover
❑ Diner's Club ❑ Eurocard ❑ JCB

Account # _____

Exp Date _____

Signature _____
(Prices in US dollars and subject to change without notice.)

PLEASE PRINT ALL INFORMATION OR ATTACH YOUR BUSINESS CARD

Name	
Address	
City	State/Province	Zip/Postal Code
Country	
Tel	Fax
E-Mail	

May we use your e-mail address for confirmations and other types of information? ❑ Yes ❑ No We appreciate receiving
your e-mail address. Haworth would like to e-mail special discount offers to you, as a preferred customer.
We will never share, rent, or exchange your e-mail address. We regard such actions as an invasion of your privacy.

Order from your **local bookstore** or directly from
The Haworth Press, Inc. 10 Alice Street, Binghamton, New York 13904-1580 • USA
Call our toll-free number (1-800-429-6784) / Outside US/Canada: (607) 722-5857
Fax: 1-800-895-0582 / Outside US/Canada: (607) 771-0012
E-mail your order to us: orders@haworthpress.com

For orders outside US and Canada, you may wish to order through your local
sales representative, distributor, or bookseller.
For information, see http://haworthpress.com/distributors

(Discounts are available for individual orders in US and Canada only, not booksellers/distributors.)

Please photocopy this form for your personal use.
www.HaworthPress.com

BOF05